**Nut:** A small component at the top of the fretboard with individual slots that space the strings evenly. Commonly made of bone or a composite.

**Output Jack:** The place you plug a guitar cable into.

**Pickguard:** Located on the body and often holds the pickups and controls for electric guitars. On acoustic guitars its typically a teardrop shaped piece of plastic found on one side of the sound hole.

**Pickup Selector:** A switch or switches on electric guitars that turns individual pickups on and off.

**Pickups:** Produce an electronic signal sent to an amplifier. There's a wide variety of pickups for both electric and acoustic guitars.

**Saddle:** A part on the bridge where the string makes contact. On electric guitars it's easily adjusted for string height and intonation. On acoustic guitars its typically white and made of bone or a composite.

**Strap Buttons:** A place on the guitar where you attach your strap.

**Strings:** Nickel strings are most common for electric guitars and phosphor bronze for acoustic guitars.

**Tuners/Tuning Keys:** Found on the headstock and used to tune the strings.

**Volume and Tone Controls:** Allows you to adjust the signal from the electronics. Found on the body of electric guitars. For acoustic guitars controls are found on the side or inside the sound hole.

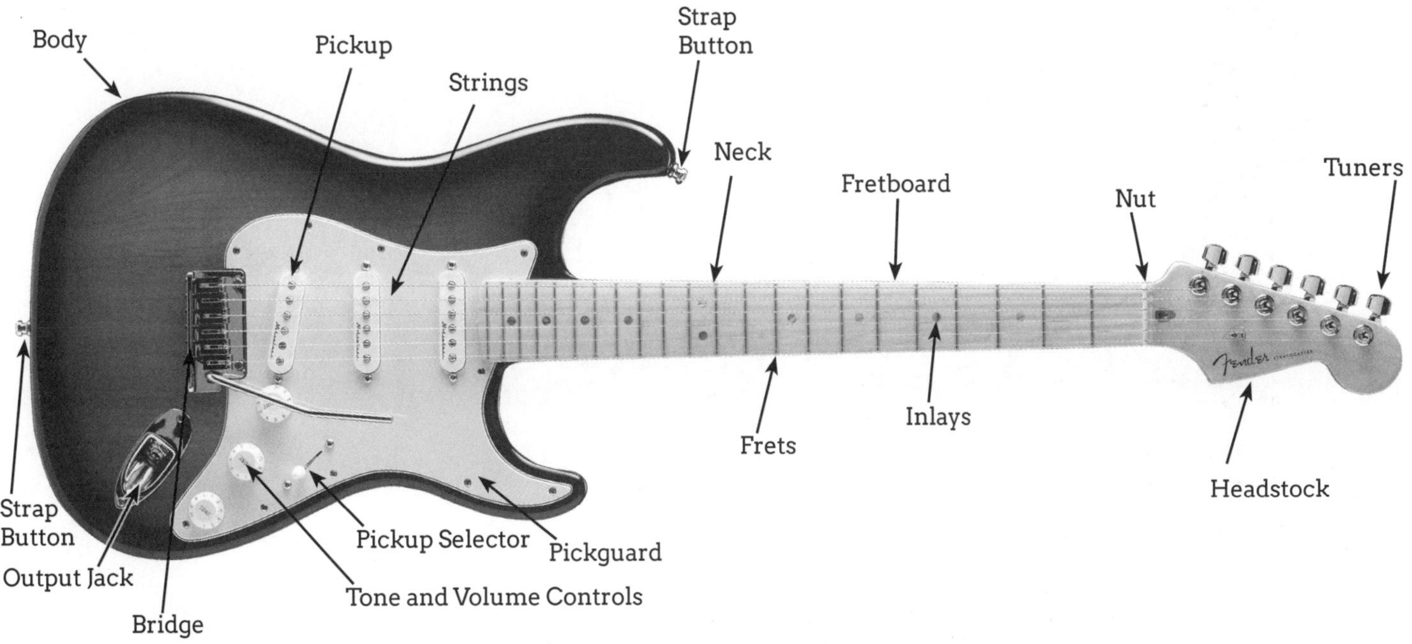

# CHAPTER 1:
# Replacing Strings

Whether it's a lone string that broke from an overly aggressive bend, or a whole set that have lost their sonic luster after being played for months, at some point, every guitarist will need to replace their strings. Each guitar type has its own unique mechanisms, but in most cases, this is an easy job. The basic idea is to get the string through the bridge and into the tuning peg. Once there, all you need to do is tune up.

Guitar strings are sold in packs, which are referred to as light gauge, medium gauge, extra light gauge, and so on. Selecting the set by the thinnest string in the pack is a common way to talk about string sets. For example, a set that has a .009 gauge for the thinnest string and a .042 gauge for the thickest string is a standard set and would be referred to as a set of .009s. While strings are typically bought in packs, many shops will also sell individual strings.

## Acoustic Guitar

### *TOOL LIST*

- ❏ Neck Rest
- ❏ String Winder
- ❏ Tuning Device
- ❏ Wire Cutters

TOOLBOX

**Selecting String Gauges**
Acoustic guitars are typically strung with phosphor bronze strings. Use light gauge (.012-.053) for a softer touch or medium gauge (.013-.056) for more aggressive picking.

1. Loosen the tuner for existing string(s). This can be done by hand or use a string winder for faster results.
2. Carefully remove the bridge pin and pull out the existing string.

3. Insert a new string into the hole. Make sure that the slotted side of the pin is facing forward toward the sound hole, and with the bridge pin about half-way down, pull the string upwards so it's seated just under the bridge. Push the pin all the way down.

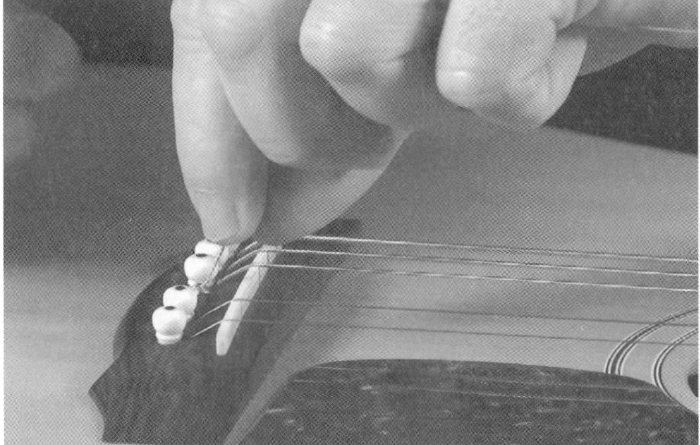
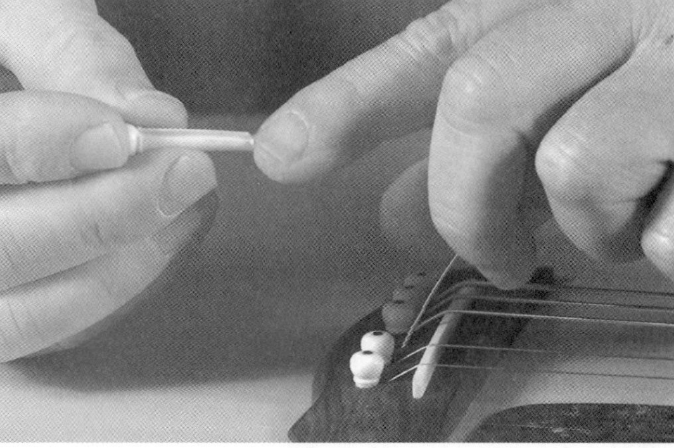

4. Slip the string through the small hole on the tuner, leaving about 4" to 6" of slack over the guitar body. Hold the string still on the tuner and wrap the string inward (toward the middle of the headstock) once around the tuning peg. While maintaining tension on the string, bend the excess part of the string upward. This will help hold the string in place when tightening.

5. Wind the string on the tuner, keeping tension on the string as it winds downward. Keeping tension on the string as you wind helps the guitar hold its tune quicker.

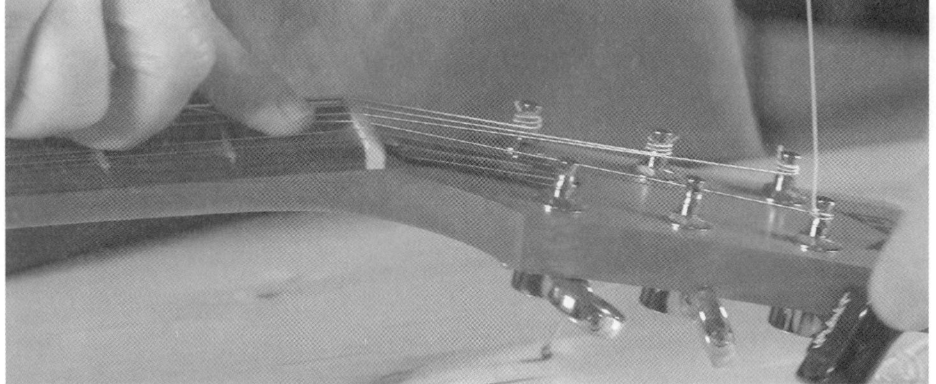

6. Slightly stretch the string while tuning to pitch. You can clip the excess string with wire cutters or wind the excess string around at the tuner until it breaks off.

**TOOLBOX**

Even if you do have perfect pitch, it's a good idea to know roughly what pitch the tuned open string should sound like. That way you don't overshoot (and potentially break a string) when tuning. A tuning device can come in handy for this purpose.

# Electric Guitar

### *TOOL LIST*

- ❏ Neck Rest
- ❏ String Winder
- ❏ Tuning Device
- ❏ Wire Cutters

TOOLBOX

**Selecting String Gauges**
Electric guitar string gauges are often chosen to match specific playing styles. Shredders usually prefer .009s for their ease of play. On the other hand, blues legend, Stevie Ray Vaughan would use strings as heavy as .013 for his high E—but that could be tough on your fingers and instrument. If you have no real preference, starting with a .010 gauge for the high E is a good all-around choice.

1. Remove the existing string by loosening the tuner or clipping the string with wire cutters. If using wire cutters, cut the string where the neck meets the body. Pull the string out through the bridge, and out of the tuner.
2. Feed the new string through the bridge. On Fender-type and other tremolo style guitars, this is done from the back of the guitar. On Gibson-type guitars the string will be fed through the tailpiece.

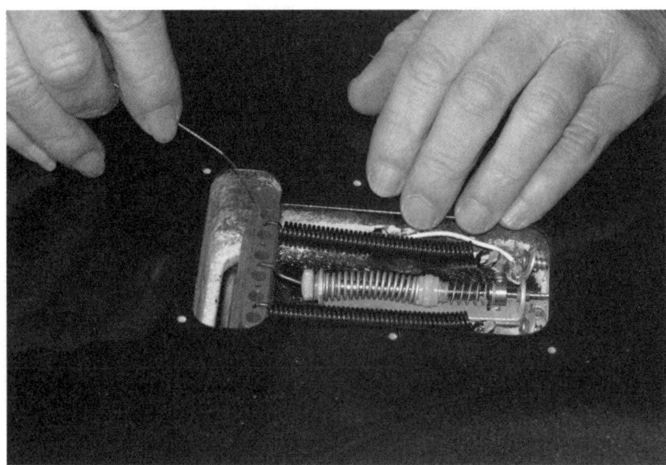

3. Clip the string about 4" to 5" past the tuner. Slip the string into the hole on the tuner leaving a little excess. Hold the string still on the tuner and wrap the string inward (toward the middle of the headstock) once around. While maintaining tension on the string, bend the excess part of the string upward. This will help hold the string in place when tightening. Ensure the string winds down and not up.

   **NOTE:** Some vintage guitars have slotted tuners. For these guitars, clip the string about 4" from the tuner and stick the string into the hole at the center of the slot.

4. Wind the string on the tuner keeping tension on the string as it winds downward around the tuner. Keeping tension on the string as you wind helps the guitar hold its tune quicker.

5. If your guitar has a string tree, slip the string under the string tree when there's enough tension to hold it in place. Stretch the string slightly and continue tuning.
6. Slightly stretch the string while tuning to pitch. You can clip the excess string with wire cutters or wind the excess string around at the tuner until it breaks off.

## Jazz Guitar

### *TOOL LIST*

- ❏ Neck Rest
- ❏ String Winder
- ❏ Tuning Device
- ❏ Wire Cutters

TOOLBOX

**Selecting String Gauges**
Jazz guitars which have a hollow or semi-hollow body are typically strung with medium gauge flat wound strings .013-.056. These strings help produce thick warm tones compared to the bright tone of nickel wound strings.

1. Remove the existing string by loosening the tuner or clip the string with wire cutters. If using wire cutters, first loosen the string to avoid strings flying off the guitar and the ball-end damaging the finish.
2. Insert the ball end of the string so it catches in the trapeze-style tail piece.

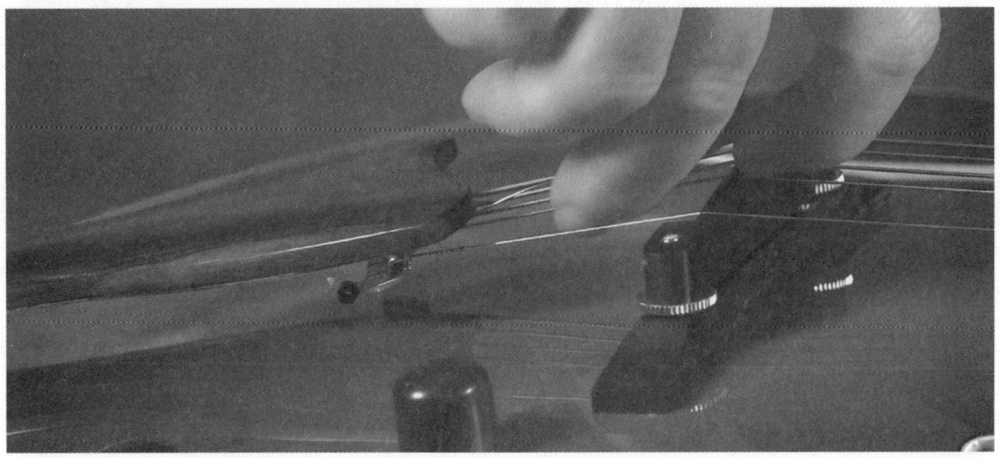

3. Slip the string through the small hole on the tuner leaving about 4" to 5" of slack over the middle of the fingerboard. Hold the string still on the tuner and wrap the string inward (toward the middle of the headstock) once around. While maintaining tension on the string, bend the excess part of the string upward. This will help hold the string in place when tightening. Ensure the string winds down and not up.

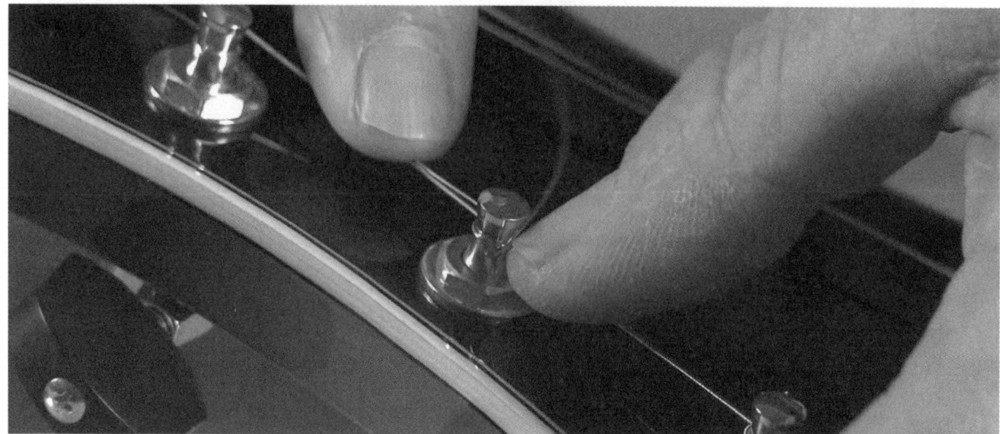

4. Wind the string on the tuner keeping tension on the string as it winds downward around the tuner. Keeping tension on the string as you wind helps the guitar hold its tune quicker.
5. Slightly stretch the string while tuning to pitch. You can clip the excess string with wire cutters or wind the excess string around at the tuner until it breaks off.

## Floyd Rose-Equipped Guitar

The Floyd Rose double-locking tremolo system is a godsend for shredders. Set up properly, a Floyd Rose-equipped guitar can be dive bombed into oblivion, and *still* remain in tune. However, this tuning stability comes with a price. When you break a string, the entire guitar goes out of tune. String changes are more complex, and repair shops usually charge more for working on them because they are labor intensive.

### *TOOL LIST*

- ❏ Allen Wrench
- ❏ Neck Rest
- ❏ Screwdriver
- ❏ String Winder
- ❏ Tuning Device
- ❏ Wire Cutters

TOOLBOX

**Selecting String Gauges**
Floyd Rose users gravitate toward string sets starting with an .009 for the high E string. Some Floyd Rose users may go slightly higher and start with a .010 but you typically won't see anything heavier.

1. Remove the three nut clamps by loosening the screw with an Allen wrench. Hold firmly as you turn in a counterclockwise motion.

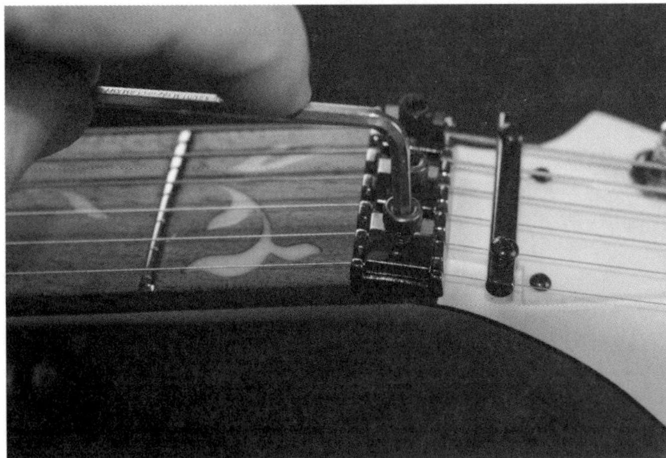

2. Loosen the set screw on the back of the bridge using an Allen wrench in a counterclockwise motion.

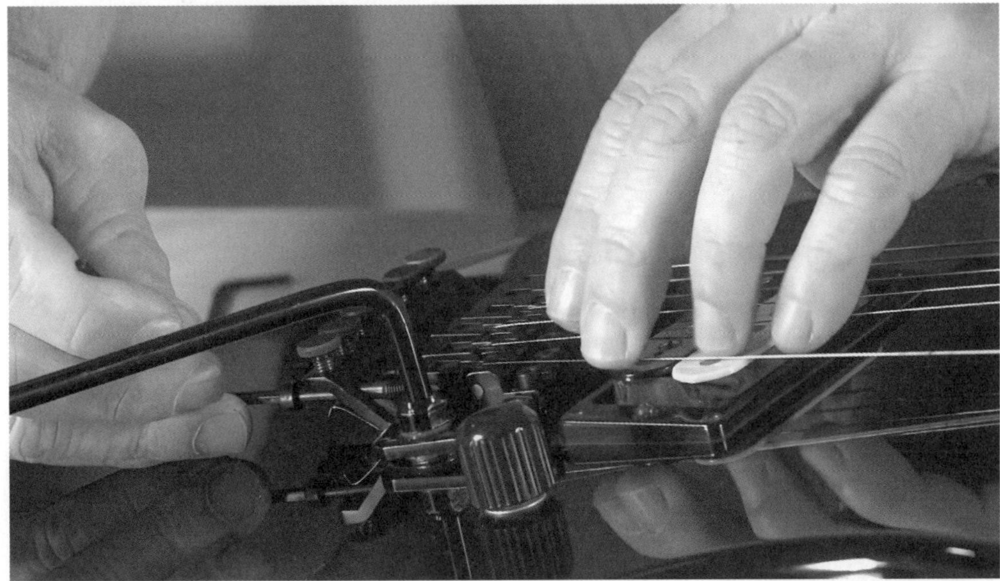

3. Pull the string out of the bridge and the tuning peg.

   **NOTE:** I recommend replacing one string at a time for Floyd Rose and tuning each new string to pitch before removing the next string. This will keep the floating bridge roughly in place and decrease time spent tuning.

4. Thread the new string through the tuning peg and under the string tree pulling it toward the bridge. Leave an extra 2" to 3" between the ball end and the tuning peg. (This is backwards compared to how you'd string a typical electric guitar.)

5. Cut the string at the bridge saddle and insert the string all the way down into the bridge saddle clamp.

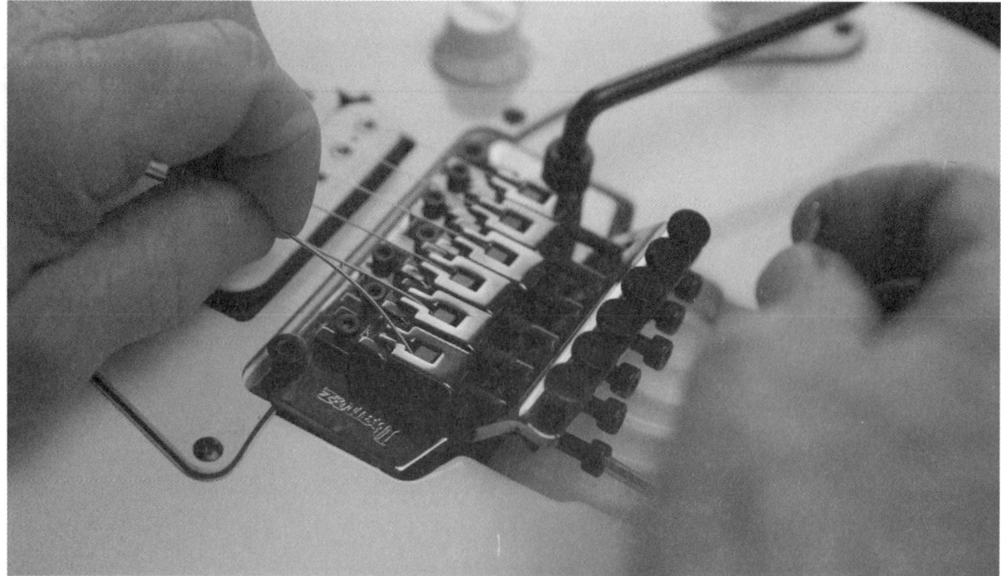

6. Do a preliminary tightening of the set screw by hand to lock the string in place. Next, insert the Allen wrench and turn clockwise to tighten. It doesn't have to be tightened excessively; it just needs to be snug.
7. Wrap the string inward (toward the middle of the headstock) once around the tuner and then continue tightening. Apply tension as you do so to ensure the string is winding down.

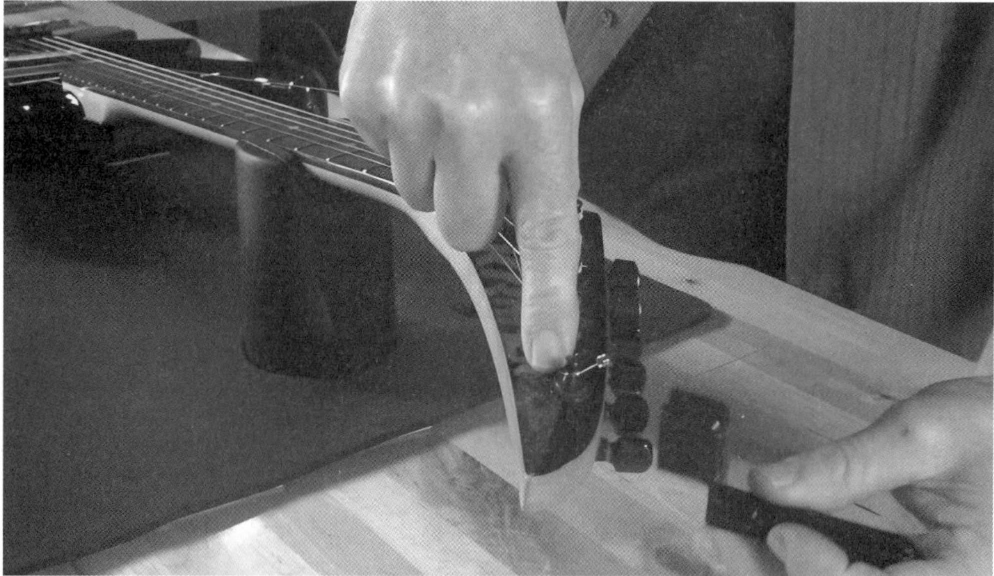

8. Reset the fine tuner at the bridge by turning it counterclockwise until it stops and then clockwise one turn. This will give you needed room for adjusting the tuning at the bridge once the strings are all locked down.

9. Once all strings have been changed, put the three nut clamps back on lightly tightening with your fingers.
10. Tune each string to pitch. Keep in mind that with the Floyd Rose floating bridge system, each string effects the others, and it will take some going back-and-forth to get the proper tuning. In other words, once one string is in tune, the others will drift out of tune so keep tuning until none of the strings need adjusting.
11. Once again, firmly tighten the three locking nuts and play the guitar aggressively, bending strings, etc., for a few minutes. Next, loosen the three nut clamps and go through the re-tuning process again.
12. Firmly tighten the three locking nuts again and from here on you'll do your tuning at the bridge with the fine tuners. If a string is slightly sharp, pull on it to stretch it and/or turn the fine tuner counterclockwise. This process of locking, unlocking, and re-locking the nut helps get your tuning to hold faster.

TOOLBOX

**Lubrication**

Use 3-in-1 oil to occasionally lubricate the knife edges on a Floyd Rose. This will help them last longer.

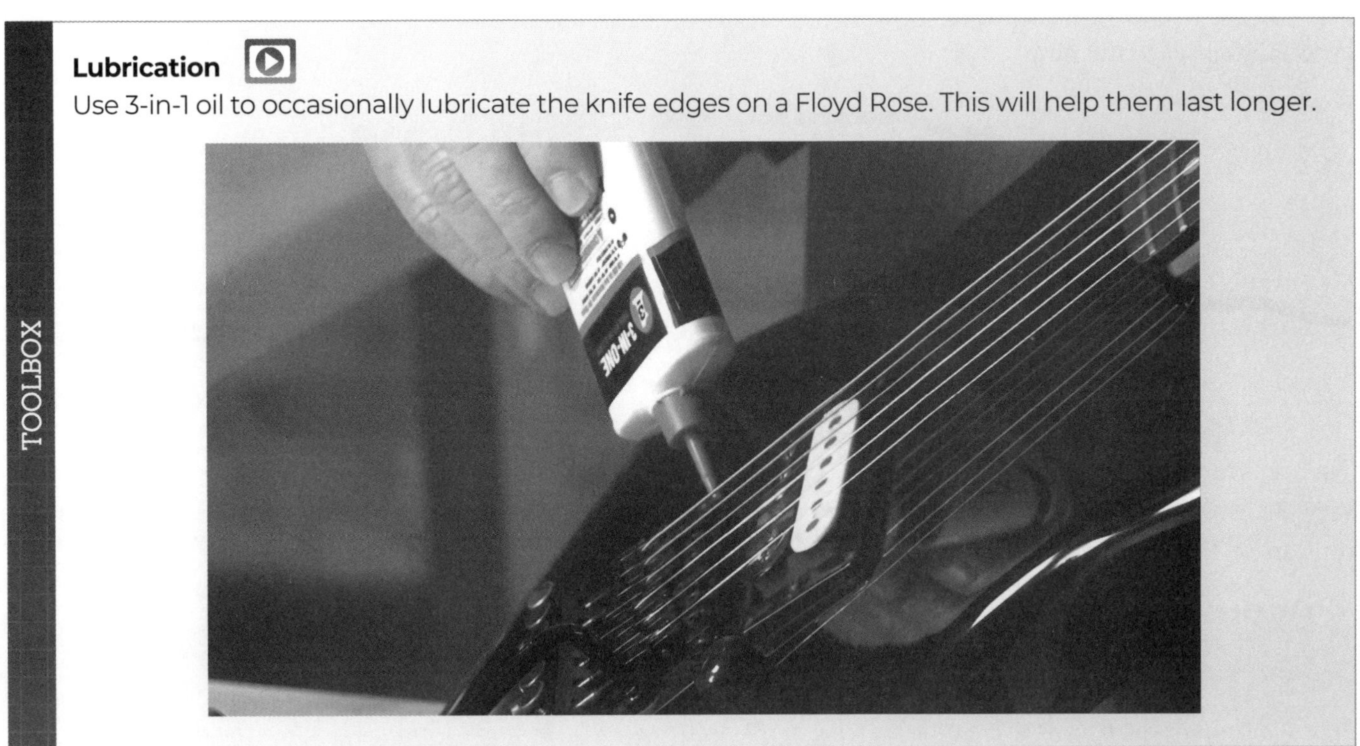

# CHAPTER 2:
## Truss Rod

A truss rod is a long metal rod that runs through the inside of the neck. Its purpose is to counter the string tension and hold the neck straight. Changes in humidity or a change of string gauge can affect a guitar neck. Adjusting the truss rod corrects this. You'll want to get the neck relatively straight, with just a crack of bow (relief).

If a neck is bowed the string action will become uneven and high off the fretboard, making the guitar difficult to play and cause tuning problems. If it's back bowed, strings will buzz or not ring out, making the guitar unplayable especially closer to the nut.

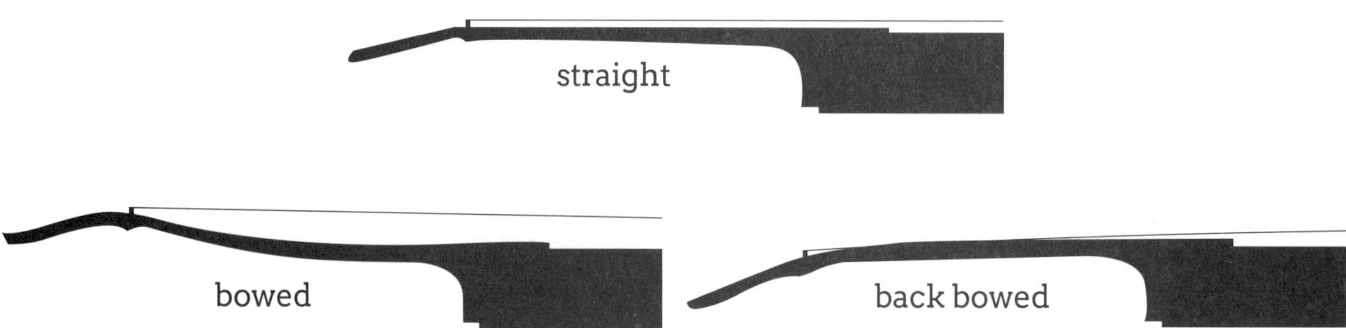


The steps for checking and adjusting the truss rod is the same for all types of guitars. However, the access point can vary. Be careful not to over tighten and break the truss rod. The process requires a firm hand; however, the truss rod can be broken or striped with too much force.

**For slide guitar, you'll want to create extra relief in the neck to get a little more clearance between the strings and frets.*

### TOOL LIST

- ❏ Business Card
- ❏ 18" Ruler
- ❏ Neck Rest
- ❏ Screwdriver
- ❏ Truss Rod Tool and/or Allen Wrench (Guitar Specific)

1. With the guitar tuned to pitch, remove it from the neck rest leaving the guitar body resting on a flat surface and the neck and headstock hanging free. Using an 18" ruler, look for a tiny gap the thickness of a business card between the ruler and the top of the 6th and 10th-12th frets.

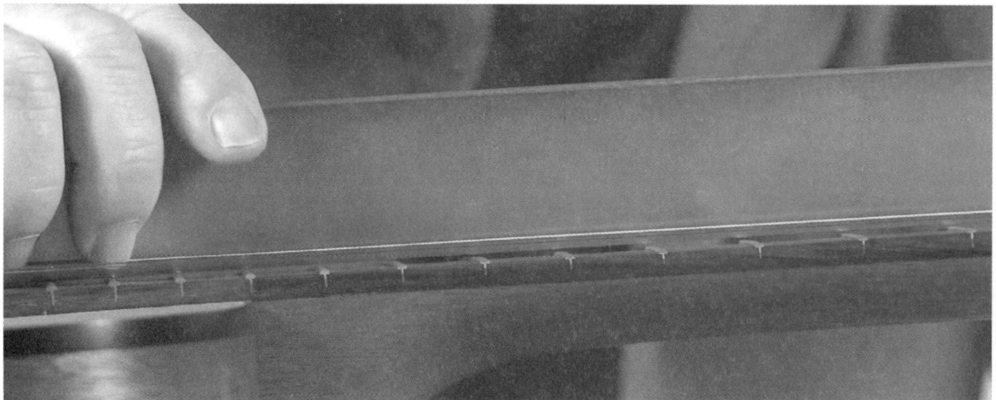

2. You'll check three zones—along the high E string, D string, and low E string. Our goal is to get the three zones as similar as possible. The neck's three zones can be slightly different however, if there's a distinct problem, like one side is back bowed and another side is bowed, you may have to take it to a qualified repair person.
3. Place the headstock in the neck rest and to start, always *loosen* the truss rod by a quarter turn (counterclockwise). If your truss rod is already tightened to the maximum, it could snap, so adjust in quarter turn increments. You can also move the D and G strings out of the nut slots to get better access.
4. If the neck has a *bow* (gap larger than the thickness of a business card), tighten the truss rod (clockwise). This brings the strings *closer* to the fretboard, counters the string tension, and straightens the neck.

   If the neck has a *back bow* loosen the truss rod (counterclockwise). This brings the strings *further* from the fretboard. Remember to always adjust in quarter turns.

5. Remove the neck from the neck rest and check your adjustment. Depending on the amount of adjustment needed the guitar neck may settle and change slightly requiring minor adjusting in a few days. It's also normal to need a truss rod adjustment after a change of season.

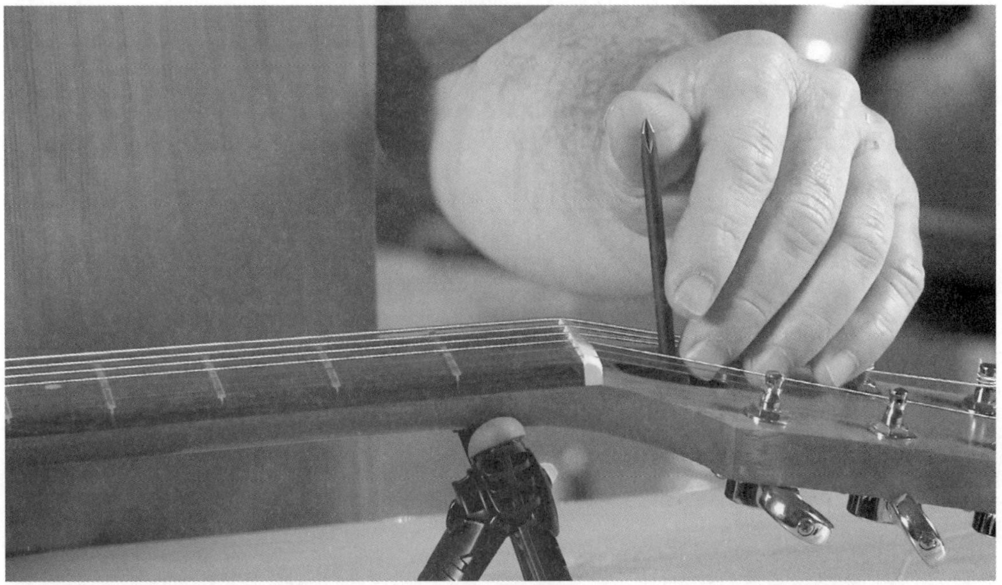

## Access Points

### Headstock of Guitar

Remove the truss rod cover at the headstock. Some guitars will require a nut driver while other instruments an Allen wrench. Be careful not to over tighten tiny screws when re-installing the truss rod cover.

## Blind Truss Rod

On many acoustic guitars, you'll access the truss rod through the sound hole. Most commonly, you'll see a hole in the brace under the fingerboard where the truss rod is located. On others, you'll need to reach inside the sound hole where you'll access the truss rod through the neck block directly under the fingerboard. Most require an Allen wrench in some cases you'll need a nut driver or socket to make adjustment.

## Guitars Requiring Neck Removal

1. Loosen all strings and clamp them using a capo around the 4th fret. This will keep the strings from tangling when removing the neck for adjustment.
2. Turn the guitar over and remove the screws from the neck plate.

   **NOTE:** Some bolt-on necks use different lengths of screws because of the shape of the neck joint, so be sure to re-install them properly.

3. Turn the guitar right side up, while keeping the neck in place.

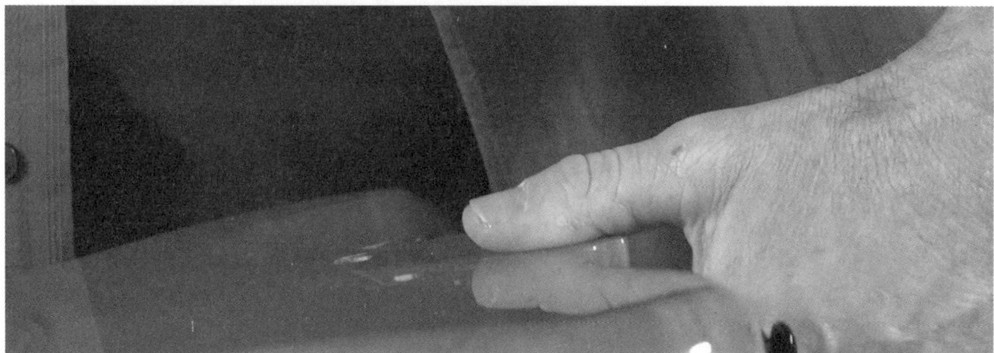

4. Slide the neck up so you can access the truss rod. Some necks can be very tight so carefully lift back and forth easing the neck out to avoid damaging the finish.

5. Whether correcting for "bow" or "back bow," always loosen the truss rod slightly before making needed adjustments and work in quarter turn increments.

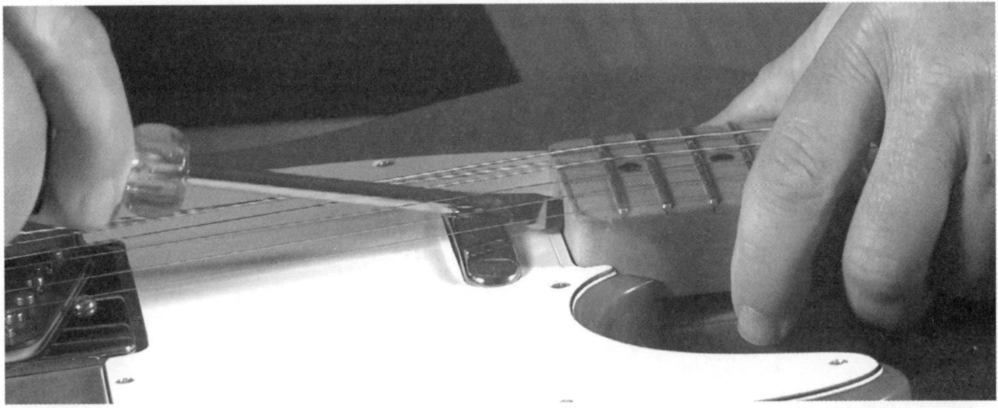

**TOOLBOX**

If your truss rod is on the tight side, spray a little WD-40 inside to loosen it.

6. Turn the guitar over, holding the neck in place as you fit the screws through the backplate again and tighten.
7. Remove the capo, tune to pitch, and recheck your adjustment.

# CHAPTER 3: Action

A guitar's action (*string height*) is the distance from the strings to the fret and refers to how the strings feel when you play. In other words, how hard it is to press the strings against the frets. A *hard action* has a greater distance between the strings and the frets. A *light action* has a closer distance and requires a lighter touch to play. How hard you pluck the strings is an important factor and will dictate how light you can set the action. Finding the right balance for your style of playing is key. I've included some typical setup measurements but don't hesitate to experiment and figure out what feels best for your playing style.

The action should be adjusted *after* the truss rod is set, and is done first at the bridge followed by adjustments at the nut.

## String Height at the Neck Joint

### Acoustic Guitar

#### TOOL LIST

- ❑ Capo
- ❑ 80-grit Sandpaper
- ❑ Neck Rest
- ❑ Pliers
- ❑ 6" Ruler
- ❑ String Winder

1. Put a capo on the 1st fret with the headstock hanging free off the work surface. This helps you get accurate measurements at the saddle as some of the strings at the nut might be higher than others since it hasn't been adjusted yet.
2. Measure the string height at the neck joint from the top of the fret to the bottom of the string. If the gap is *too wide*, you'll *lower* the height of the strings by sanding the saddle. If the gap is *too small*, you'll either need a new saddle or shim the current one. (This process is the same as shimming the nut, see page 23.)

   A gap measuring 3/32" on the high E string and 7/64" on the low E is considered a *medium action* for acoustic guitar. A gap of 5/64" for the high E string and 3/32" for the low E string is considered a *light action*.

   A proper saddle radius makes a smooth transition from string to string. You'll need to maintain the saddle radius when adjusting so you create an even, balanced action across the fingerboard. DO NOT adjust height for strings individually but rather the overall saddle radius.

3. Remove the capo and loosen all strings. Pull the bridge pins out and remove strings from the bridge. Wrap the strings in groups of three to keep them out of the way.
4. Remove the saddle and be sure to mark the bottom of the saddle to match with the high and low strings so you can put the saddle back exactly as it was.

TOOLBOX

If the bridge pins or saddle are stuck, use a pair of pliers to carefully pull them out. Always use two hands when doing this.

5. Copy the radius of the saddle with a pencil creating a reference mark as a guide. You'll estimate how much to remove to achieve the desired action height. Using 80-grit sandpaper placed on a hard flat surface, sand down the saddle. Keep in mind, less is more as you can't put material back.

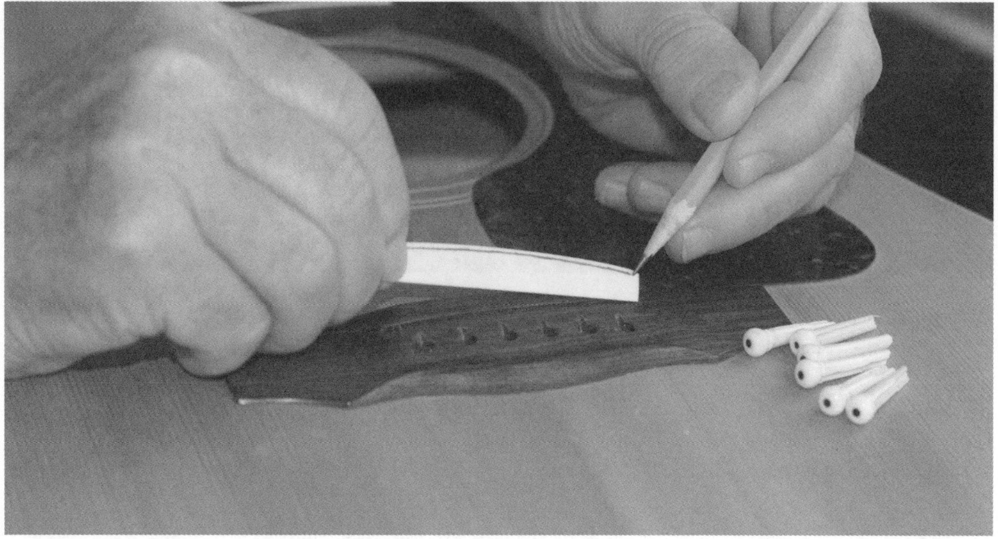

6. Slip the saddle back into the bridge, re-string the guitar, and tune to pitch. To make sure the saddle is stable and even across ranges, tune up the middle strings first—rather than the outer strings. Put the capo back on the 1st fret and recheck your measurements. Repeat these steps as needed. This job may necessitate going back and forth many times to get it right.

TOOLBOX

**Piezo Pickups**
Guitars with piezo pickups are best restrung by first tuning middle strings G and D, followed by B and A, and then the two E's. This helps keep even pressure on the pickup as you tune the strings.

If your guitar has a piezo pickup, make saddle adjustments from the *top only*. Piezo pickups sit under the saddle and require a perfectly machined surface for accurate sound to be reproduced, and messing with the bottom surface can result in a noticeably uneven string response when played through an amplifier.

## Electric Guitar

### *TOOL LIST*

- ❏ Allen Wrench
- ❏ Capo
- ❏ Neck Rest
- ❏ 6" Ruler

1. Put a capo on the 1st fret with the headstock hanging free off the work surface. This helps you get accurate measurements at the saddle as some of the strings at the nut might be higher than others since it hasn't been adjusted yet.

2. Measure the string height at the neck joint from the top of the fret to the bottom of the string. A gap measuring 1/16" on the high E string and 1/16" for the low E string is considered typical for rockers. Blues players like a little extra room to grab and wail, so 5/64" for high E string and 5/64" for the low E string is standard.

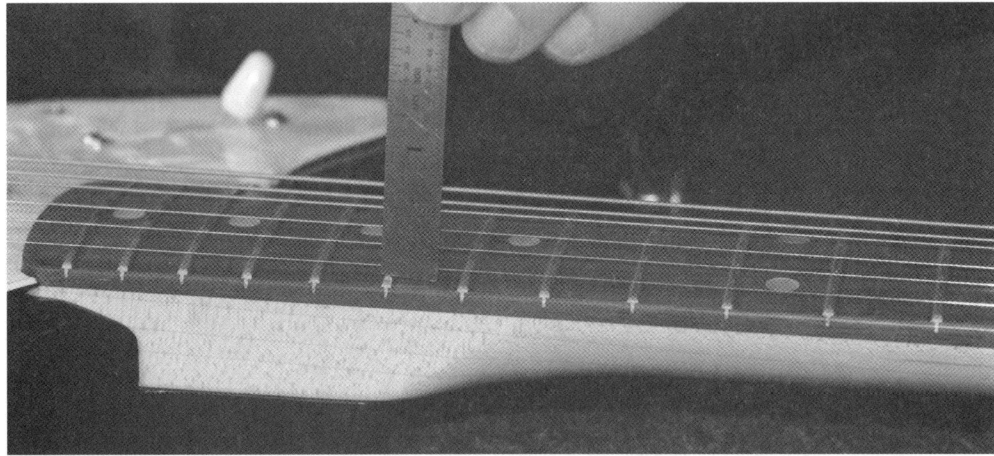

3. Adjust the bridge saddles with an Allen wrench moving in half-turn increments. Turn the Allen wrench clockwise to raise the string height and counterclockwise to lower.

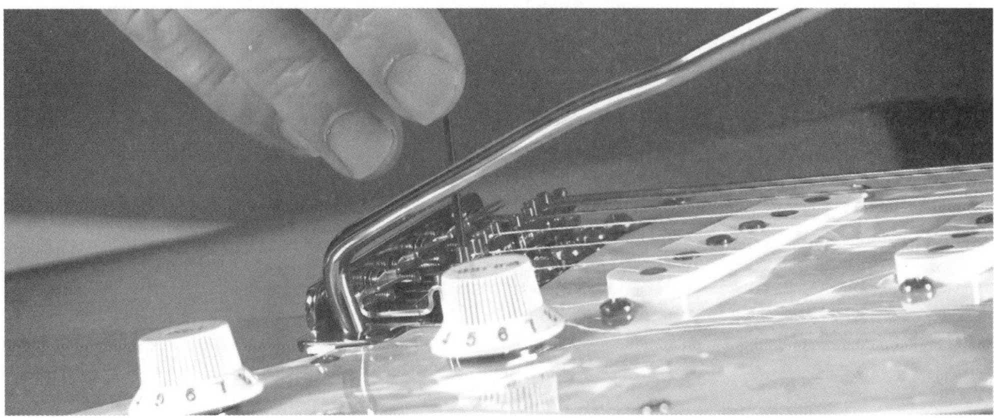

4. Recheck your measurement at the neck joint and adjust matching the fingerboard radius. Repeat the process as necessary.

## Jazz Guitar

For jazz guitar, we first make course adjustments by changing the height of the bridge, and then fine adjustments by filing individual string slots.

***TOOL LIST***

- ❑ Capo
- ❑ Neck Rest
- ❑ Nut Files
- ❑ 6" Ruler

1. Put a capo on the 1st fret with the headstock hanging free off the work surface. This helps you get accurate measurements at the saddle as some of the strings at the nut might be higher than others since it hasn't been adjusted yet.
2. Measure the string height at the neck joint from the top of the fret to the bottom of the string. A gap measuring 1/16" on the high E string and 1/16" for the low E string is typical for jazz guitar.

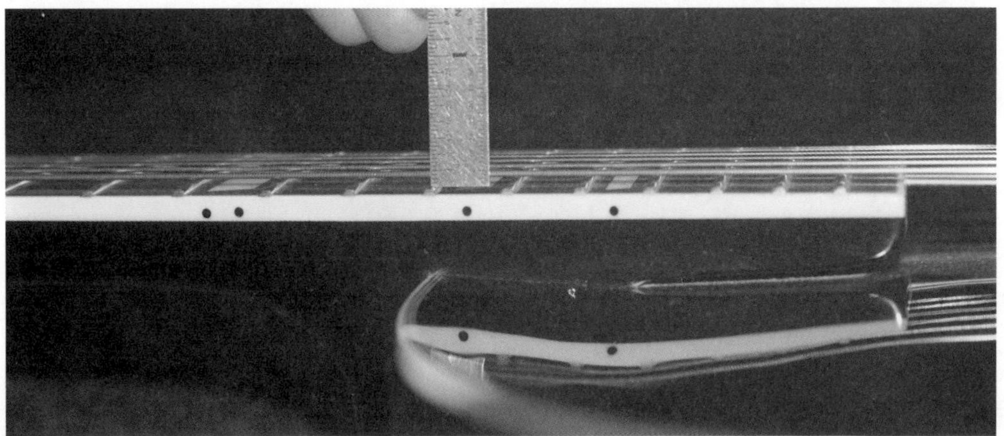

3. Get your strings close to the desired range with raising or lowering the bridge by turning the thumbscrews on the bridge. These can be difficult to turn so you may need to loosen the string tension.
4. If there are individual strings that don't match the desired string height, you'll have to adjust them. Strings that require adjustment need to be higher than the others as you can only adjust the string downward. In other words, if one string is lower than a 1/16" and all the other strings are correct, you'll have to raise the bridge until the individual string that's too low measures 1/16". This will throw off the other strings and you'll have to adjust them back down to 1/16".
5. Using a nut file, adjust the notch in tiny increments. Be sure the string is seated all the way down in the notch before measuring again. String slots are meant to be shallow notches and if a bridge requires more than a slight adjustment to the notch you might want to bring it to a professional.

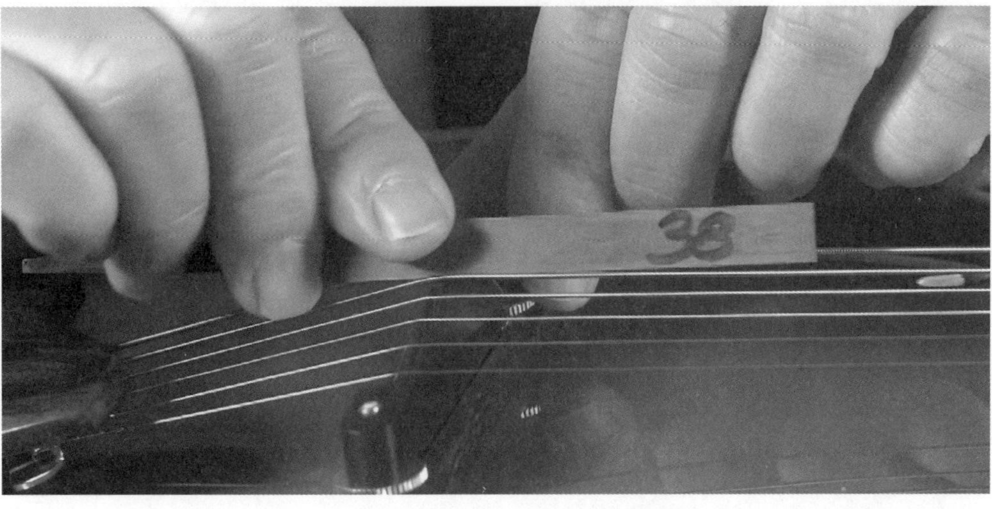

6. Once you've matched the radius (1/16" for all strings at the neck joint), you can raise or lower the overall height of the action with the thumb screws by adjusting either side up or down. The strings over the fingerboard will remain balanced.

## Slide Guitar 

Slide guitar necessitates a higher action along with a much larger radius at the bridge. We'll adjust a typical electric guitar to accommodate the needs of a slide player.

**NOTE:** This adjustment is for guitars with individual adjustable saddles.

### *TOOL LIST*

- ❏ Allen Wrench
- ❏ Capo
- ❏ Neck Rest
- ❏ 6" Ruler

1. Put a capo on the 1st fret with the headstock hanging free off the work surface. This helps you get accurate measurements at the saddle as some of the strings at the nut might be higher than others since it hasn't been adjusted yet.
2. Lay a ruler across the strings to get a sense of the radius. You don't have to get the bridge radius totally flat but you will need to create a surface that is almost flat (large radius) where the ruler rocks just slightly

**Too Much Curvature:**

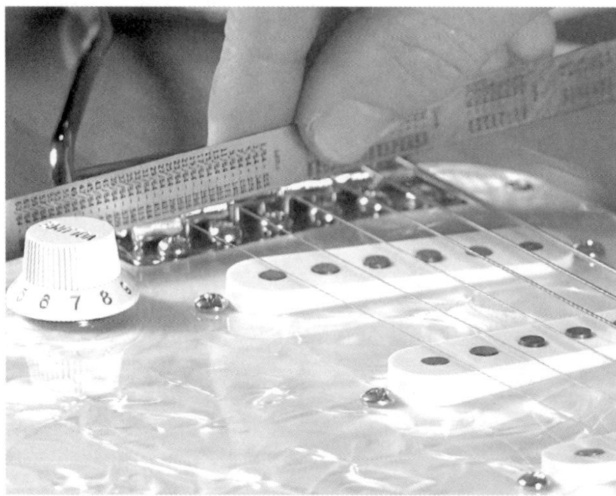

**Good Curvature:**

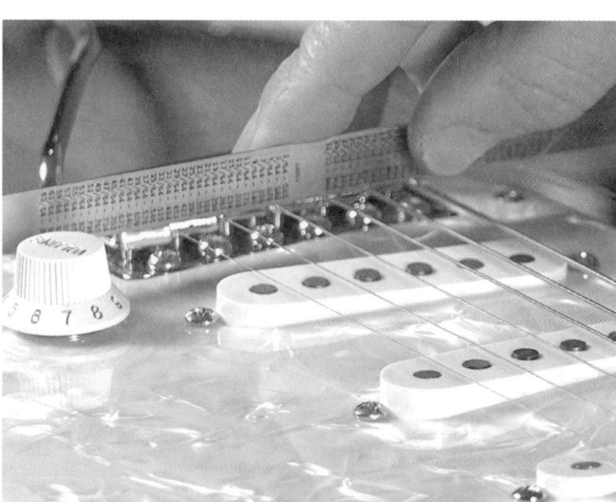

3. Using an Allen wrench, adjust the outer strings, bringing the height up to 3/32" at the neck joint. Turn the Allen wrench clockwise to raise the string height and counterclockwise to lower. If your guitar allows, lower the middle-string saddles to 5/64".

   With your ruler laying across the strings, adjust the B string so the ruler touches the high E, B, and G string simultaneously. Do the same with the A string until the ruler touches the D, A, and low E string simultaneously. You'll now have a slight rocking motion when checking with the ruler across all the strings. This setup allows for normal fretting as well a slide.

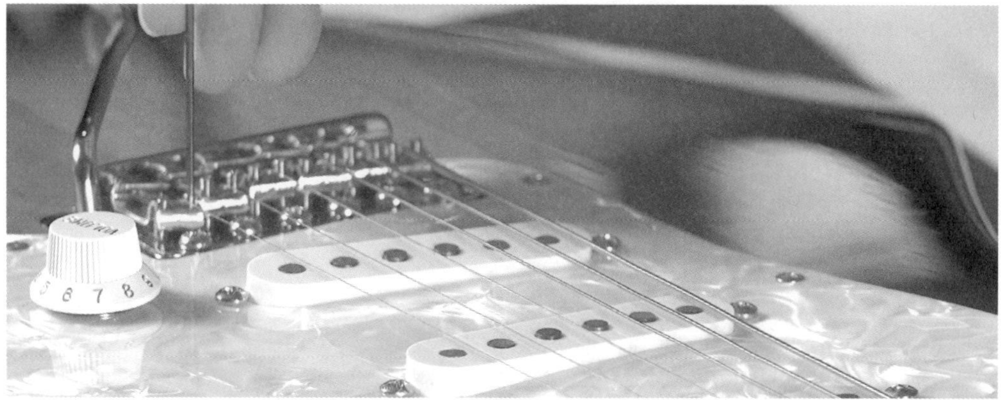

4. Recheck your measurement at the neck joint and repeat the process as necessary.

## String Height at the Nut

The proper string height at the nut creates clearance over the 1st fret when playing the open strings and is important for balanced playability and intonation. This gap is too small to measure with a ruler, so I'll show you a technique using touch and your eye to make the adjustment.

### Testing for String Height at the Nut

Press an open string down at the 1st fret several times to get a feel for the string height.

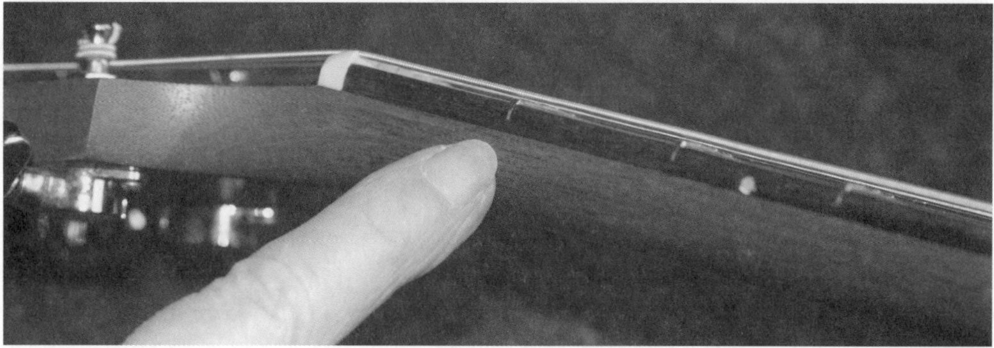

Next, holding the string down at the 1st fret, make note of the gap over the 2nd fret. The gap at the 2nd fret is a good representation of what the gap should be for the open string over the 1st fret when adjusting the nut. While still holding the string down at the 1st fret, touch the string a few times right on top of the 2nd fret to get a feel and look at the gap.

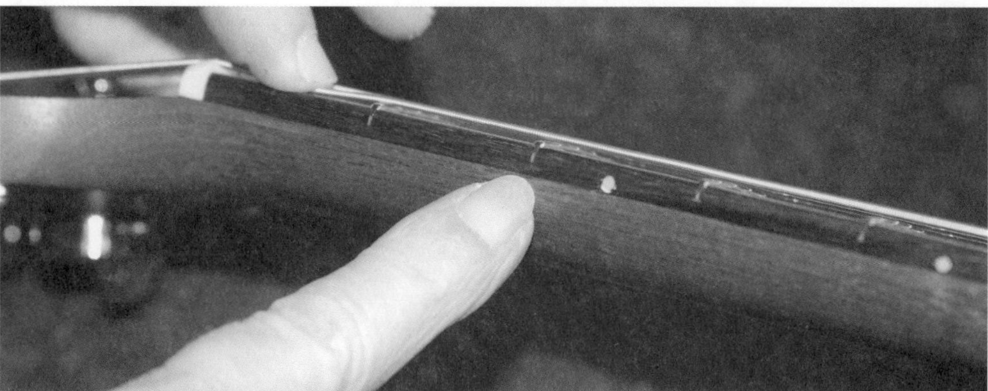

If the string height at the 1st fret is *too high,* use nut files to *lower* the string height, bringing the string closer to the fret. If the string height at the 1st fret is too *low,* shim the nut to raise the string height, bringing the string further from the fret.

When shimming, you'll need to determine which string(s) are the lowest and then create a shim which brings the lowest string(s) up to the proper height. The other strings will then need to be adjusted using nut files.

> **TOOLBOX**
>
> If there is fret buzz when lightly plucking the open string, this is also a sign that your nut is too low for that string and should be shimmed.

## Lowering String Height with Nut Files

The process for acoustic, electric, and jazz guitar is the same.

### *TOOL LIST*

- ❑ Nut File Set

1. Check each string's height at the nut using the method described in *Testing for String Height at the Nut,* starting at the high E. Remember, if the string height at the 1st fret is too high, you'll use nut files to lower the string height, bringing the string closer to the fret.
2. Loosen the string a few turns and take the string out of the nut. Using a file that matches the string's gauge or is slightly wider, move the file in a back-and-forth motion and against the sides as you file. Only do a little at a time and check your progress frequently; you can't undo if you take too much off.

3. Put the string back into the nut slot and check the string height again. Ensure the string is settling all the way down into the slot each time you put the string back into the nut slot. Moving the file side to side a touch while filing helps alleviate this issue.
4. Once the string is at the desired height, take a nut file one size lower and run it through the slot, very softly, at the center of the nut groove. This will eliminate any of the pingy, sitar-like sound that can happen when plucking open strings.
5. Once both the bridge and nut have been adjusted, measure the string height without a capo to check playability. When the capo is removed, expect the measurements to be slightly higher. Tune to pitch and play every note on the guitar, re-doing steps as necessary.

## Raising String Height with a Shim

It is common to raise the nut height of a guitar that is primarily used for slide.

### *TOOL LIST*

- ❑ Block of Wood
- ❑ Exacto Knife
- ❑ Hammer
- ❑ Miniature Slotted Screwdriver
- ❑ Neck Rest
- ❑ Shim Stock/Business Card
- ❑ 6" Ruler
- ❑ String Winder
- ❑ White Glue

**NOTE:** This is a tricky adjustment. If you're not comfortable with this procedure, bring it to a qualified repairperson.

1. Check each string's height at the nut using the method described in *Testing for String Height at the Nut*. If the string height at the 1st fret for any of the strings is too low, you'll shim the nut. This will raise the string height bringing it to the proper height further from the fret.
2. Loosen all strings, take them out of the tuning pegs, and move them out of the way.
3. With an Exacto knife, hold it with a slight angle and score the top and sides of the nut. This removes the bond from the finish. Rotate the guitar in the neck rest as you score different sides to maintain support.

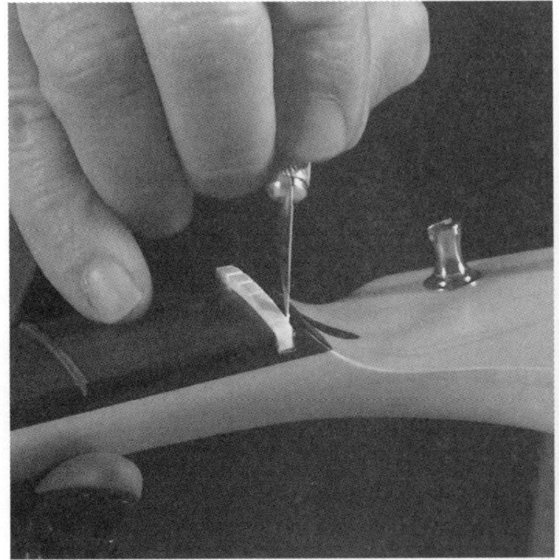
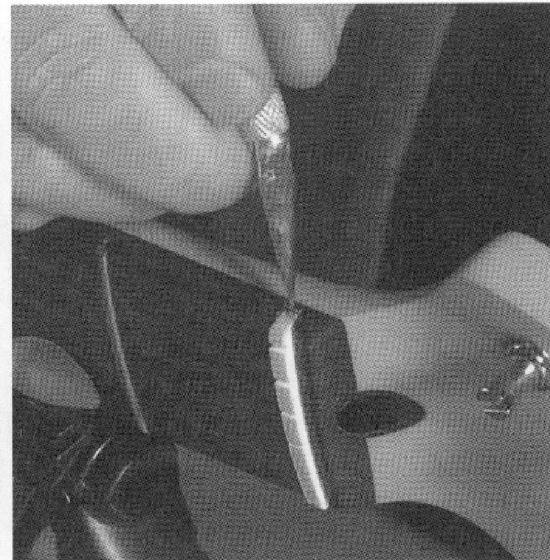
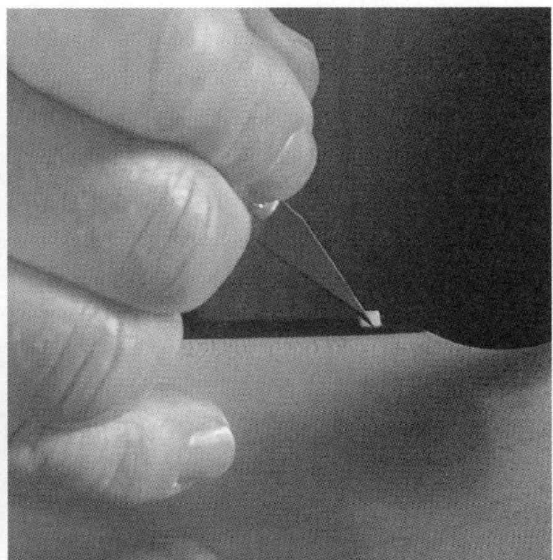

4. Hold a small block of wood at an angle on top of the nut and tap it a few times from the front and then the back with a hammer. You don't have to hit it too hard. The light taps send a shock that should loosen up the nut.

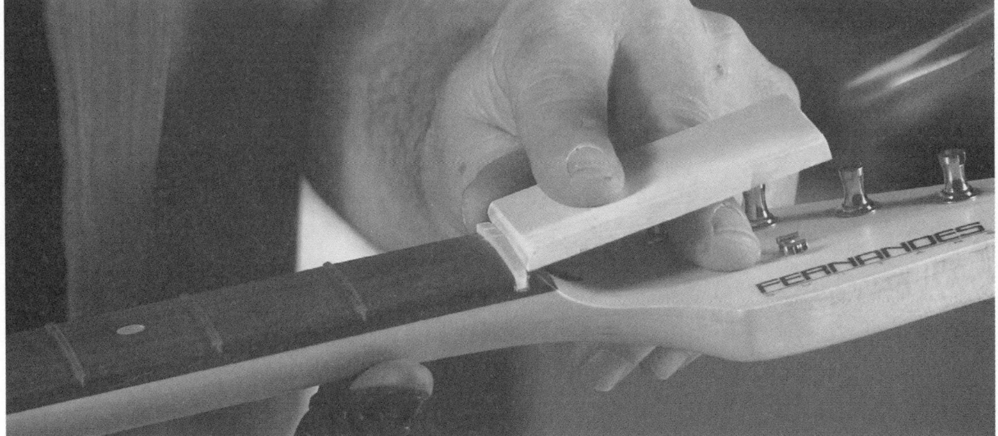


**TOOLBOX**

Depending on what type of glue was used to secure the nut it may not come out easily—Super Glue or Epoxy can make for a tough removal. If that's the case, it's safest to bring to a qualified repairperson.

5. Tip the guitar sideways, place a miniature slotted screwdriver on the high E side of the nut, and gently tap it with the hammer upward and out of the slot. Use small, light taps; don't force it.

6. Shim the nut using shim stock (a non-glossy business card will do). Put white glue on the nut and place the nut atop the shim stock. Use an Exacto knife to cut off excess. This needs to be precise to properly fit back into the nut slot.

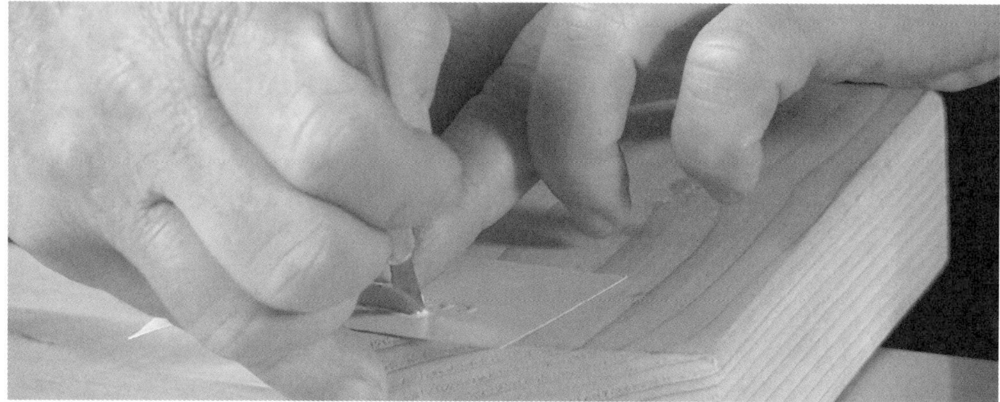

7. Wipe off any excess glue and slip the shimmed nut back into position. DO NOT glue it into the nut slot at this point.
8. Restring and check the height at the nut, filing if necessary. (See *Lowering String Height with Nut Files.*) Once all the strings are good remove the nut, add a touch of white glue, and reinstall it. Tighten the two E strings and realign the nut from side to side making sure there is an equal amount of space from the string to the edge of the fretboard on both sides. Wipe off excess glue and tune it up.

## Floyd Rose-Equipped Guitar

Floyd Rose guitars have a significantly different process for adjusting the action at the bridge and nut.

### String Height at the Neck Joint

Like a jazz guitar, we make course adjustments by changing the overall height of the bridge, and fine adjustments by using shims.

***TOOL LIST***

- ❏ Allen Wrench
- ❏ Capo
- ❏ Floyd Rose Shims
- ❏ Neck Rest
- ❏ 6" Ruler

1. Put a capo on the 1st fret with the headstock hanging free off the work surface. This helps you get accurate measurements at the saddle as some of the strings at the nut might be higher than others since it hasn't been adjusted yet.
2. Measure each string's height at the neck joint from the top of the fret to the bottom of the string. A gap measuring 1/16" on the high E string and 1/16" gap on the low E string is typical for a Floyd Rose setup.
3. Set the bridge so that all strings measure 1/16" or lower. Depending on the type of bridge mounting studs, use a slotted screwdriver or an Allen wrench to adjust the overall height. Turn counterclockwise to raise and clockwise to lower.

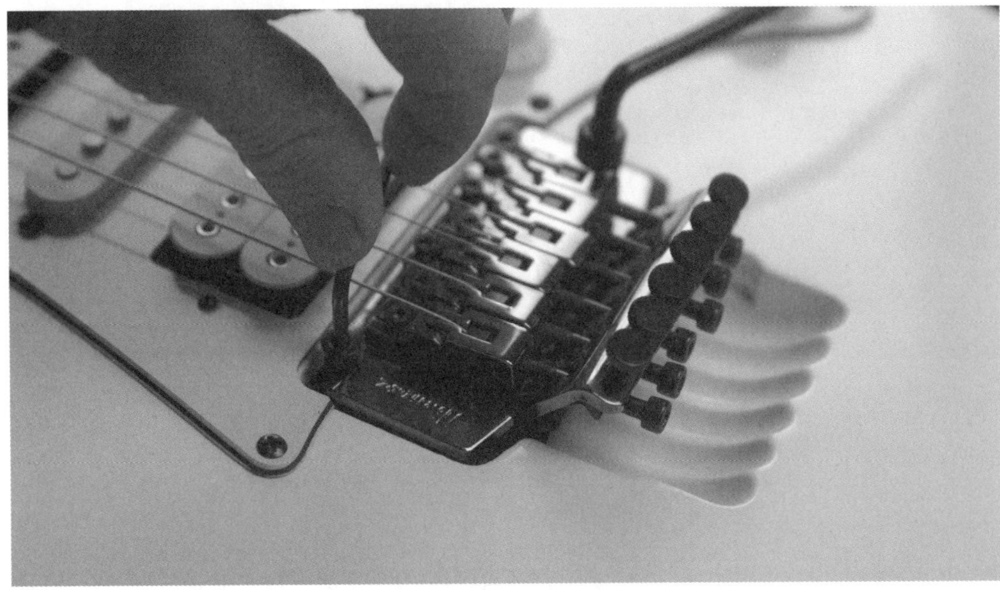

4. For strings that don't match the fingerboard radius, we'll use shims to change the height of individual strings.

> **TOOLBOX**
>
> Saddle shims are made specifically for Floyd Rose setups. These have a hole designed to fit the set screw and come in different thicknesses. You can purchase these at a guitar specialty store.

5. To install a shim, remove the capo and loosen the string. Next, put the capo back on and remove the set screw holding the saddle in place.

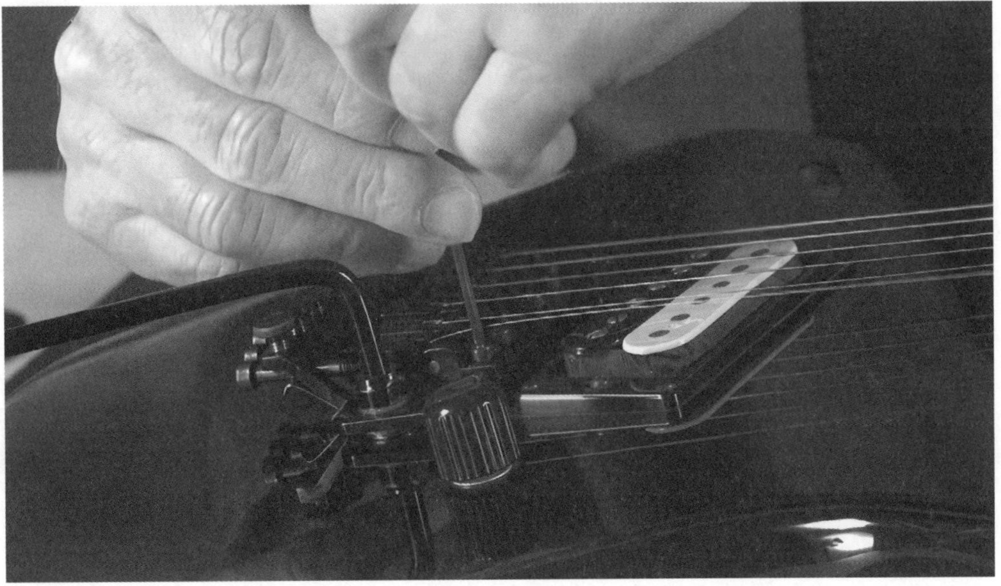

6. Lift the saddle up (with the string still locked in place), slip the shim under, and tighten the set screw holding the saddle where it had been.

7. Remove the capo and tune the guitar to pitch. Put the capo back on, measure, and repeat the process adding more shims as needed.

## Raising String Height at the Nut

**NOTE:** If the strings are too high at the nut, bring the guitar to a qualified repairperson as a precision cut into the wood will be needed to bring the nut down to the proper height.

### *TOOL LIST*

- ❏ Allen Wrench
- ❏ Exacto Knife
- ❏ Neck Rest
- ❏ Pliers
- ❏ Shim Stock/Business Card

1. Check the string height at the nut using the method described in *Testing for String Height at the Nut.*

   If the high E, B, or G string is too low, shim from the high E side of the nut. If the low E, A, or D string is too low, shim from the low E side of the nut. Again, if the strings are too high at the nut, I would suggest bringing it to a qualified repairperson as a precision cut into the wood will be needed to bring nut down to the proper height.
2. Pre-cut a shim (a business card works) matching the width at the outside edge of the nut and making it about 2" long in case you need to double it up to increase the shim height.
3. Depending on the type of locking nut, you will either need to loosen the two screws securing the nut from the top or, flip the guitar over and loosen the screws through the back of the headstock running through the neck.

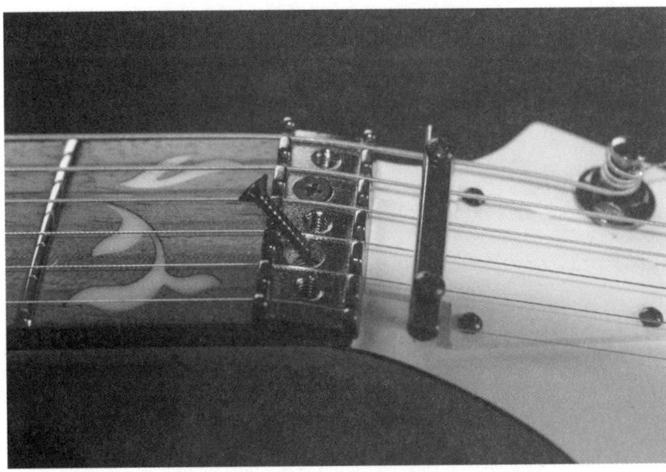

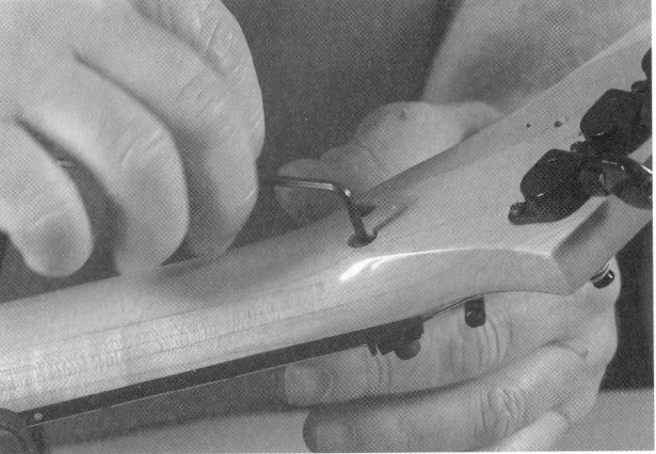

4. Let's assume the E, G, or B string is too low. With the guitar resting on the neck rest, install the locking nut bolt for the high E string and grip it with pliers. While lifting the nut, slip the shim under the nut about a 1/4" from the edge. Check the new gap at the 1st fret for all the strings. Leave excess shim hanging out during this process.

TOOLBOX

**Working with Shims**
After adding a shim, you'll find other strings have been effected in the process. To find the correct balance for all strings, you may need to experiment with adjusting the thickness of shims from one side or the other.

5. Tighten the set screws that secure the locking nut and check if any further adjusting is needed.

   **NOTE:** All the strings are affected each time you shim, so check every string looking for the best overall balance.

6. Cut the excess shim material off with the Exacto knife.
7. Tune the guitar to relative pitch. Stretch out the strings, re-tune as needed, and clamp down the nut. Continue to pull and stretch the strings, even employing the whammy bar if desired, for 10 to 15 minutes. Then, unclamp the nut and re-tune the guitar. Take it out of the neck rest as you tune (it does make a little bit of a difference). Once you are in tune, clamp it and you are done! From this point on do all your tuning with the fine tuners on the bridge.

# CHAPTER 4:
# Intonation

Correct intonation refers to fretted notes on the fingerboard playing *in tune.* If the intonation is off, a properly tuned string will play in tune on the first few frets but as you play further up the fingerboard, say the 12th fret, the note will play out of tune. In other words, the note will be flat or sharp at the 12th fret. When a guitar is intonated properly, every note on the guitar will be in tune.

Action height, frets, string gauge, and the length of string from the nut to the saddle all come into play when adjusting the intonation. It's important to follow steps from the chapters on adjusting the *Truss Rod* and *Action* before starting work on intonation.

When adjusting intonation, the goal is to make the harmonic on the 12th fret the same pitch as the fretted note on the 12th fret. To do this, you'll shorten or lengthen the strings at the bridge area. If the fretted note is *flat* compared to the harmonic, you'll make the string *shorter.* If the fretted note is *sharp* compared to the harmonic, you'll make the string *longer.*

**NOTE:** Electronic tuners are of little use tuning your guitar if it has not been properly intonated.

TOOLBOX

After replacing strings, let your guitar sit overnight and settle before adjusting the intonation.

## Acoustic Guitar 

***TOOL LIST***

- ❏ File
- ❏ Pencil and Paper
- ❏ Pliers
- ❏ Sandpaper
- ❏ String Winder
- ❏ Strobe Tuner (A strobe tuner gives a more accurate reading, but you can use a regular tuner)

1. Tune the guitar perfectly. Hold your guitar as if you were to play normally and play the harmonic on the 12th fret. For each string, write down where the fretted note sits (sharp or flat) compared to the harmonic. Do this several times assuring you don't push the string around when fretting to achieve a clean and accurate reading. The end goal is for these pitches to match.
2. Remove the bridge pins and take the strings out. Wrap the strings into two groups of three to keep them out of the way.
3. Make a small pencil mark for each string position on the top of the saddle.

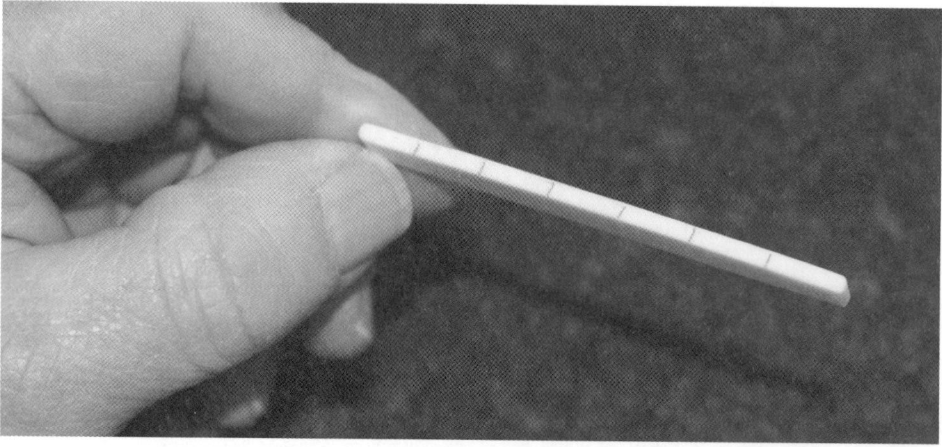

4. Remove the saddle. If it's too tight, use a pair of pliers to gently grab the end of the saddle and pull it out. Be sure to mark the bottom of the saddle for high E and low E in case you drop it and cannot differentiate.
5. Shape the saddle with a file, making changes in small increments.
   - If the fretted note is *sharp* compared to the harmonic, file the *front/neck side* of saddle. The goal is to make the string contact the saddle farther from the neck than it did before—which lengthens the string. Be careful to leave some area untouched where the string will rest on top of the saddle. This will maintain the action height you've established earlier.
   - If the fretted note is *flat* compared to the harmonic, file the *back side* of the saddle so the string makes contact closer to the front/neck side of the saddle. This shortens the string making it sharper. Be careful to leave some area untouched where the string will rest on top of saddle. This will maintain the action height you've established earlier.

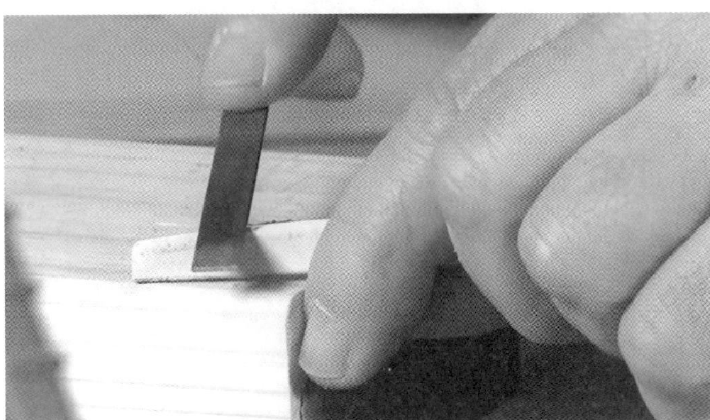
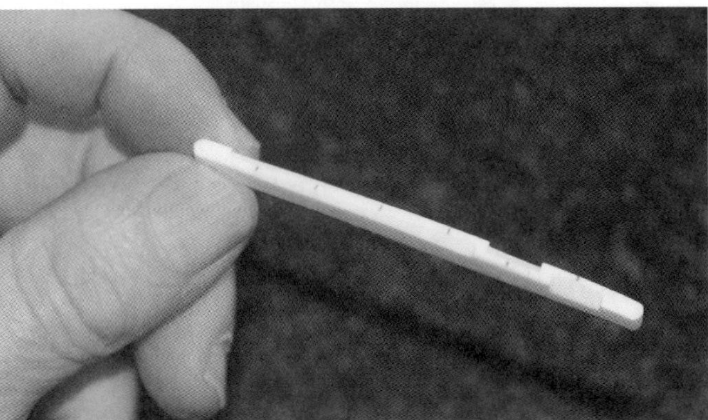

6. Smooth over the saddle with 400-grit sandpaper.

7. Put the saddle back in the bridge, re-install the strings, and check intonation. Continue adjusting as needed; it may take a couple tries to get it right.

**NOTE:** Achieving perfect intonation for acoustic guitars is not always possible and may require moving the saddle slot position. I suggest contacting a professional repair person to do this work.

## Electric Guitar

### *TOOL LIST*

- ❏ Pencil and Paper
- ❏ Screwdriver
- ❏ Strobe Tuner (A strobe tuner gives a more accurate reading, but you can use a regular tuner)

1. Tune the guitar perfectly. Hold your guitar as if you were to play normally and play the harmonic on the 12th fret. For each string, write down where the fretted note sits (sharp or flat) compared to the harmonic. Do this several times assuring you don't push the string around when fretting to achieve a clean and accurate reading. The end goal is for these pitches to match.

2. If the fretted note is *flat* compared to the harmonic, make the string shorter by *moving the saddle forward* (turn counterclockwise). If the fretted note is *sharp*, make the string longer by *moving the saddle back* (turn clockwise).

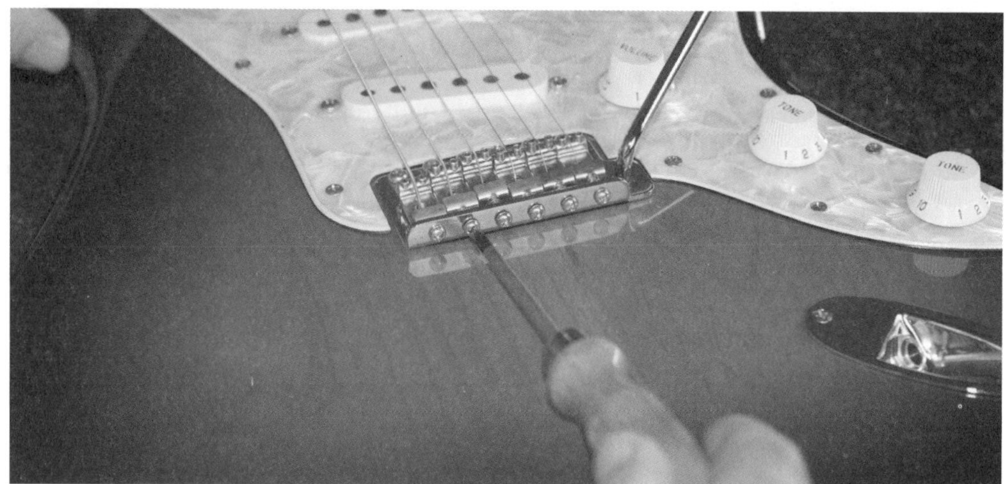

3. Re-tune and compare the harmonic to the fretted note again. Repeat for each string.

## Jazz Guitar

### *TOOL LIST*

- ❏ Pencil and Paper
- ❏ Masking Tape
- ❏ String Winder
- ❏ Strobe Tuner (A strobe tuner gives a more accurate reading, but you can use a regular tuner)

1. Using masking tape and a pencil, lightly mark the bridge position. This will help when estimating how much to slide the bridge forward or backward to correct the intonation.

2. Tune the guitar perfectly. Hold your guitar as if you were to play normally and play the harmonic on the 12th fret. For the high and low E strings, write down where the fretted note sits (sharp or flat) compared to the harmonic. Do this several times assuring you don't push the string around when fretting to achieve a clean and accurate reading. The end goal is for these pitches to match.

3. Loosen the A, D, G, and B strings a few turns each to take pressure off the bridge.
4. Adjust both E string positions at the same time by grasping the archtop bridge and sliding it slightly *forward* toward the neck if the string was *too flat* or *backward*, toward the bottom of the guitar if the string was *too sharp*. Be careful to keep outside strings aligned side to side with the fingerboard.
5. Re-tune and continue adjusting until you've matched the fretted note and the harmonic for both high and low E's. Doing this will re-align a properly tempered bridge to play in tune.
6. For bridges with individual strings that need further adjustment, follow the steps for *Acoustic Guitar Intonation*. If your archtop guitar has a tune-o-matic style bridge, follow the steps for *Electric Guitar Intonation*.

## Floyd Rose-Equipped Guitar

***TOOL LIST***

- ❏ Allen Wrench
- ❏ Pencil and Paper

1. Tune the guitar perfectly. Hold your guitar as if you were to play normally and play the harmonic on the 12th fret. For each string, write down where the fretted note sits (sharp or flat) compared to the harmonic. Do this several times assuring you don't push the string around when fretting to achieve a clean and accurate reading. The end goal is for these pitches to match.
2. If the fretted note is *flat* compared to the harmonic, *make the string shorter* by loosening the string at the tuner a few turns and using an Allen wrench to loosen the small setscrew for the saddle. Slide the saddle forward a little making the string shorter. Tighten the setscrew and tune the string.

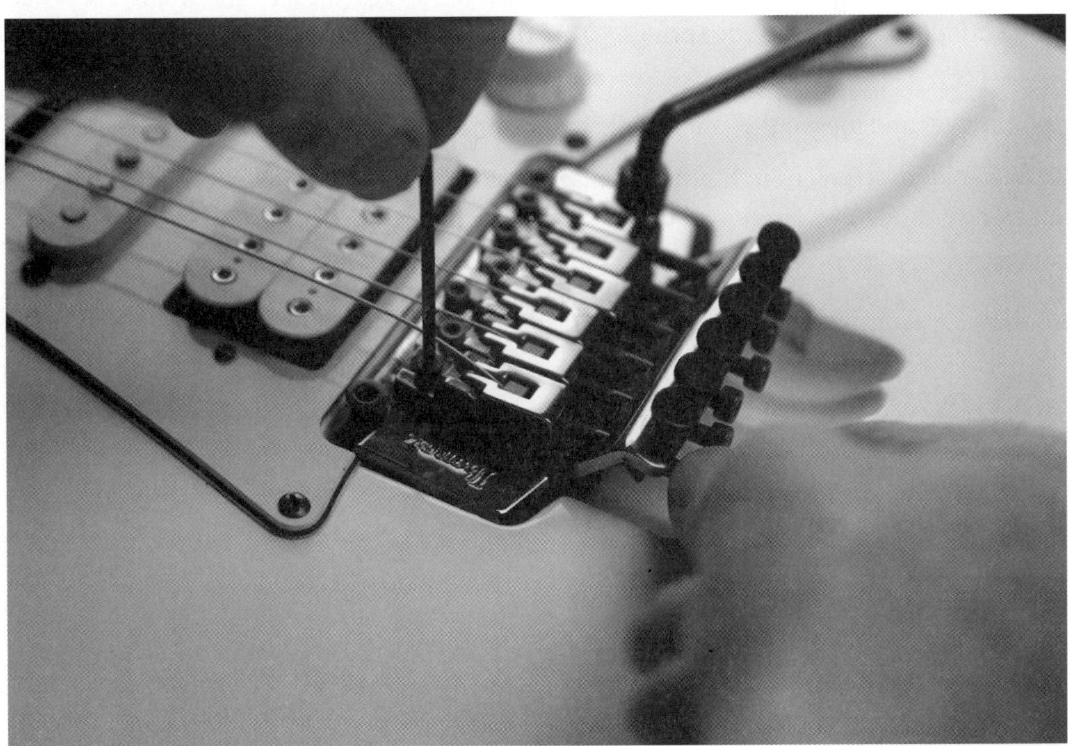

3. Conversely, if the string was *sharp*, slide the saddle back toward the bottom of the guitar *making the string longer*. Tighten the setscrew for the saddle and tune the string.
4. Re-tune and compare the harmonic to the fretted note again. Repeat for each string.

# CHAPTER 5:
# Tremolo Bridge Adjustment

Traditional Fender-style tremolo bridges can be adjusted to work as a *floating tremolo* or a *fixed tremolo/bridge (hard tail)*. A floating bridge allows you to raise and lower pitches with the whammy bar. There can be tuning issues when playing with a floating bridge, and for guitarists who would like to avoid the tuning problems and do not use the tremolo all that much, a nice compromise is setting the bridge in a fixed position.

**NOTE:** Many guitars will come from the manufacturer with five springs installed in the back of the guitar. If you plan to use the tremolo at all, you will need to remove two of those springs.

## Electric Guitar, Floating Tremolo

Floating the bridge is a balancing act between string tension and spring tension. It allows for that tremolo effect when using the tremolo bar—sometimes referred to as a whammy bar.

***TOOL LIST***

- ❑ 6" Ruler
- ❑ Screwdriver
- ❑ Tuning Device

1. Remove the backplate cover and check to see there are three springs. If there are five, you will need to remove two. Keep the middle and two outside springs. Using three springs works well when playing with .009 or .010 gauge strings.
2. Turn the guitar over and loosen the four middle strings until the bridge lies flat on the body of the guitar.
3. Adjust the four middle screws by tightening until the head of the screw touches the bridge and then backing off one full turn so the screws are close, but not actually touching the bridge.

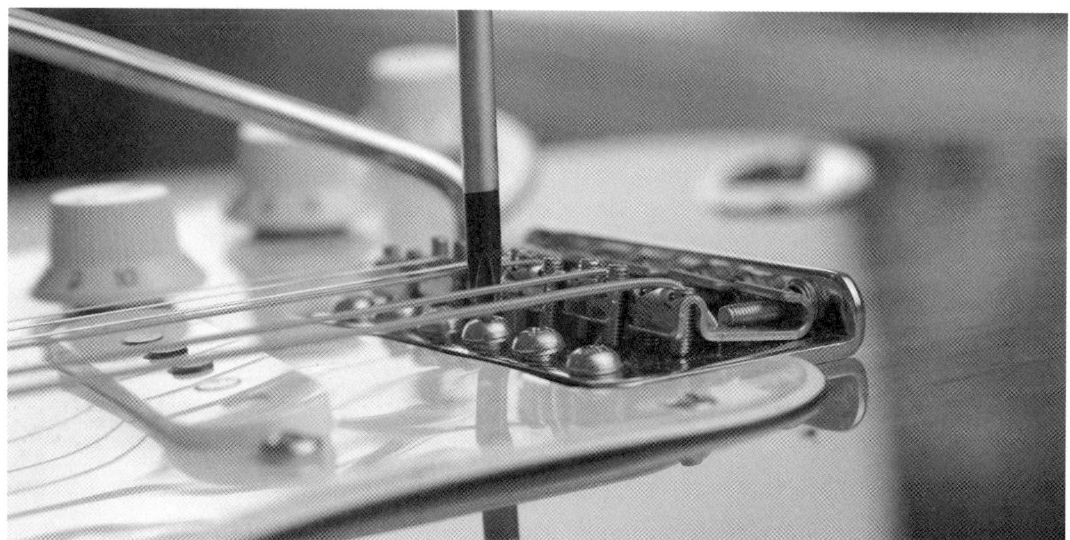

4. Adjust the outside screws so they just barely contact the bridge. Be sure when adjusting the outside screws that the bridge continues to lay perfectly flat on the top of the guitar.

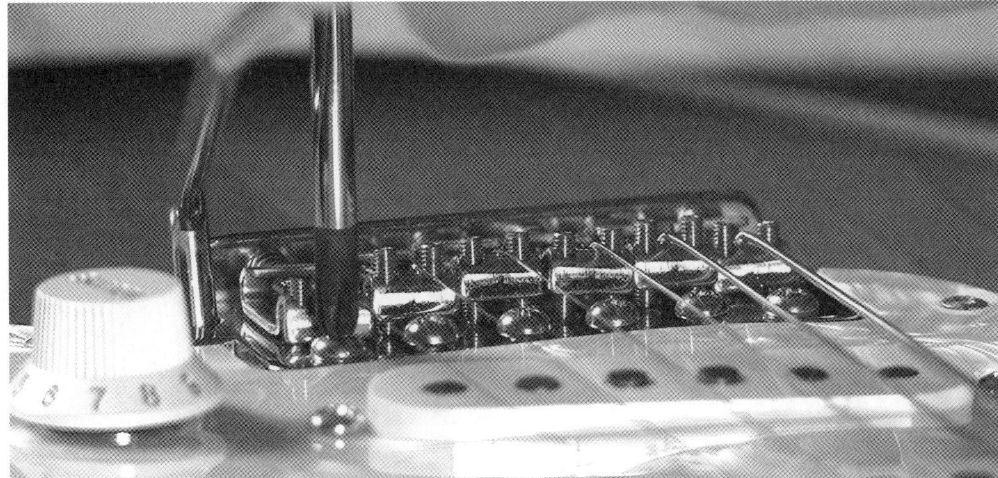

5. Re-tune the strings; you may need to do this a couple times until it settles in.
6. With a 6" ruler, check the tilt at back of the bridge. The back side of the bridge should tilt up from the string tension. A tilt of 3/32" at the highest point will give the B string a good half step rise in pitch when pulling up on the tremolo bar. For players looking to just waiver chords occasionally, a tilt measuring anywhere from 1/16" to 3/32" will do.

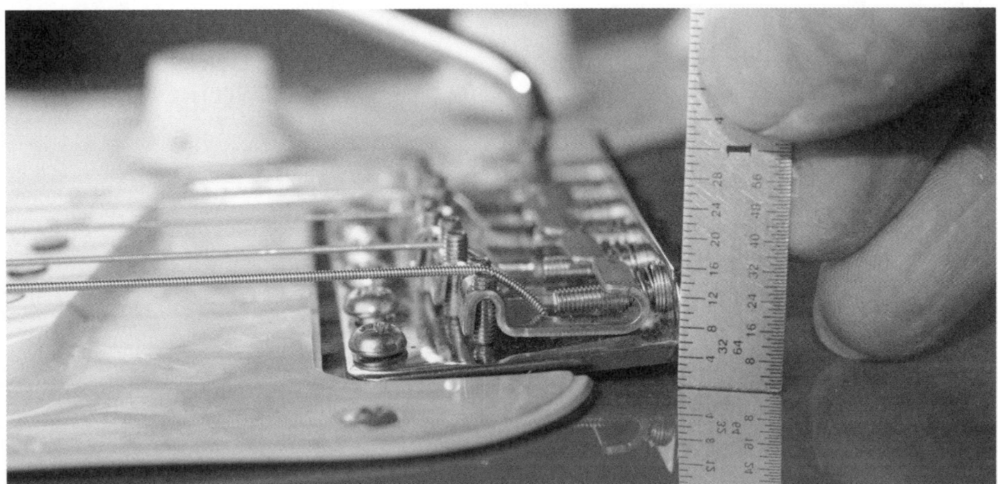

7. To adjust tilt, loosen or tighten the screws on the tremolo spring claw working in half and quarter turns to add or remove tension from the springs.

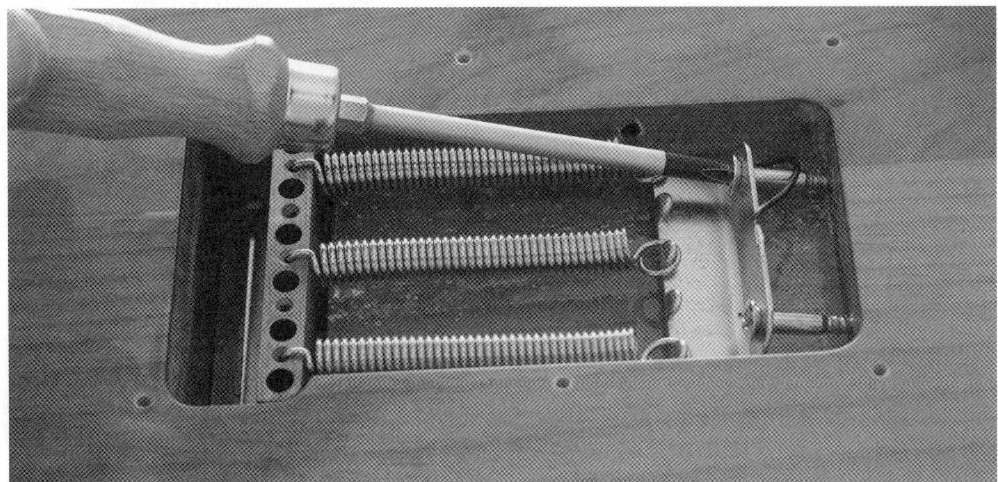

8. Turn the guitar over and retune until all strings are holding their pitch. Check the measurement and adjust as necessary.

9. To remedy the inherent tuning issues created by strings binding at the nut, use graphite or teflon tape.

TOOLBOX

**Balancing Act**
Getting the bridge to float in the best position for your style will require repeated adjusting of the spring tension and of course re-tuning each time. But once it's dialed in, you're finished and no further adjustments are needed. If you change string gauge, you'll need to complete this adjustment again.

## Electric Guitar, Fixed Tremolo

Some players love the standard Fender-style tremolo bridge but rarely use the tremolo bar and prefer to minimize the tuning issues. If this fits your style, the bridge will need to lay flat on top of the guitar. This adjustment will allow you to do those sweet country bends while holding a second note in tune.

***TOOL LIST***

- ❏ 6" Ruler
- ❏ Screwdriver
- ❏ Tuning Device

1. Remove the backplate and check to see that there are three springs. If there are five, you will need to remove two. When playing with .009 or .010 gauge strings, the three springs will have the needed muscle to lay the bridge flat on top of the guitar. Using just three springs also allows you to maintain a nice feel with the tremolo bar when you do reach for it.
2. With the guitar tuned to pitch, adjust the screws on the tremolo spring claw on the back of the guitar until the bridge lays flat.

3. Re-tune the strings and check to see if bending the B string up a half step on the fingerboard will cause the bridge to move. If the bridge moves, even a small amount, tighten the spring claw. Make small quarter to half turns on the screws until the bridge holds in place when bending the B string sharp. You're looking for just enough spring tension to hold the tremolo bridge in place while still maintaining soft enough spring tension to easily use the tremolo bar.

## Floyd-Rose Equipped Guitar

The Floyd Rose bridge should be level with the top of the guitar when it's tuned to pitch. The knife edges holding the bridge against the posts are meant to be in this position when the tremolo bar is not in use. If it's set at an angle, the tremolo's knife edges won't work optimally and will have a hard time maintaining the tuning.

**Incorrect Bridge Angle:**

**Correct Bridge Angle:**

***TOOL LIST***

- ❏ Screwdriver
- ❏ Tuning Device

1. Remove the backplate and check to see that there are three springs. Using three springs works well when playing with .009 or .010 gauge strings. If you prefer an extra slinky feel, you can get away with two springs when playing with .009s or lighter.
2. Adjust the two screws on the tremolo spring claw working in half and quarter turns to add or remove tension from the springs until the bridge is parallel to the body.

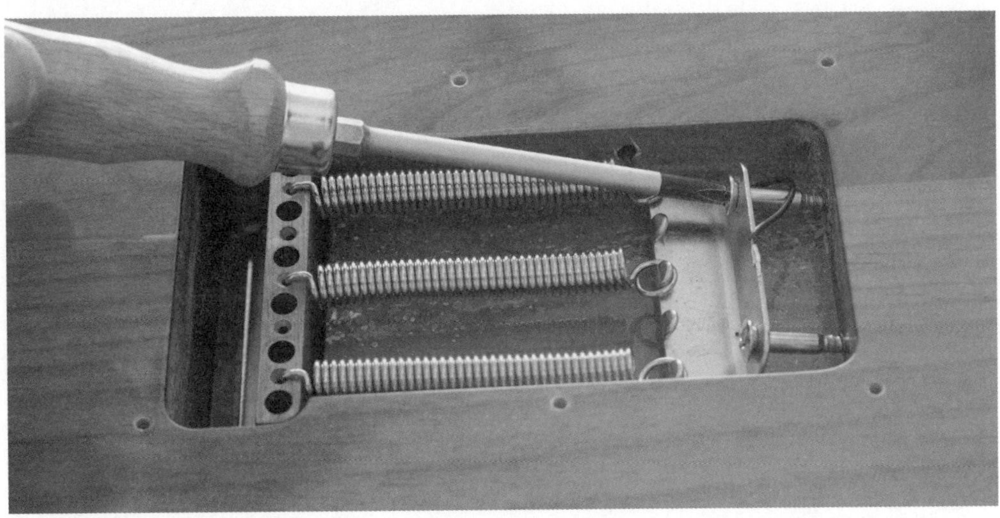

3. Turn the guitar over, and retune until all strings are holding their pitch. Getting the bridge to float in the proper position will require repeated adjusting of the spring tension and of course re-tuning each time. But once it's dialed in, you're finished and no further adjustments are needed. If you change string gauge, you'll need to complete this adjustment again.

# CHAPTER 6:
# Pickup Height

The pickup height (the distance between the strings and the pickups), has a great effect on the tone and output of your guitar. If a pickup is too close, the magnetic field is strong enough to alter the string's vibration and effect the sustain and tuning. If the pickup is too low, you may not have enough output.

The goal is to fine-tune the tone as well as achieve a balance between the neck, middle, and bridge, or whatever pickup configuration you have. It's a simple adjustment that can make a noticeable difference. Use a ruler and the measurements provided as a starting point. With the guitar plugged into the amplifier, you'll need to use your ear to make the final adjustments.

## Electric Guitar

***TOOL LIST***

- ❏ Screwdriver
- ❏ 6" Ruler

1. While holding the strings down at the neck joint, measure the distance from the pickup to the bottom of the string. Measurements may vary based on type of pickups and musician's personal preference but here are some middle-of-the-road measurements to get you started:

| Single Coils | Treble Side | Bass Side |
|---|---|---|
| Bridge pickup | 3/32" | 3/16" |
| Middle pickup | 3/32" | 3/16" |
| Neck pickup | 1/8" | 5/32" |
| **Humbuckers** | | |
| Bridge pickup | 5/64" | 3/32" |
| Neck pickup | 1/8" | 1/8" |

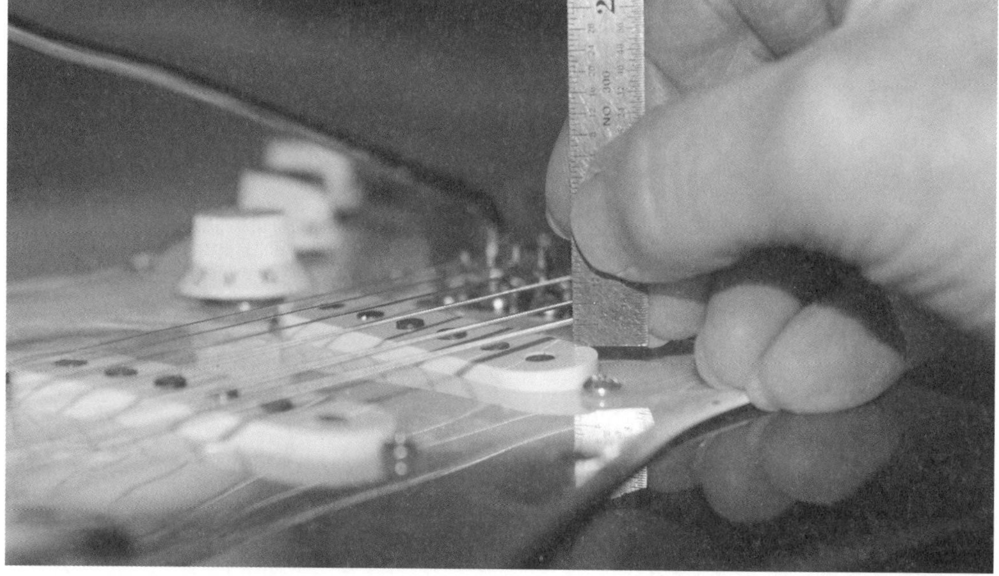

2. Using a screwdriver, adjust the screw for pickup height. Be aware there are limits on how far the pickup will adjust up or down. You can strip the screw if you tighten too much. If you loosen too far, the screw may detach from the pickup.

3. Recheck with the guitar plugged into the amplifier. Switch between individual pickup positions and strum the guitar. At this point, use your ear to adjust the output balance. Having a similar output balance in the individual pickup mode will give best results when pickups are switched into the combination mode (two pickups on at the same time). This is subjective and guitars often use unbalanced sets, so play around with it and find what flavor fits your style.

TOOLBOX

With single coil pickups, be careful how close the pickup gets to the strings. Too close and it can pull on the string, causing it to sound out of tune when playing higher up on the fingerboard.

**NOTE:** Many humbucker pickups have the option to fine-tune the string-to-string balance. The output differs depending on the type and gauge of strings you use. If a string is too loud, adjust the corresponding screw further away from the pickup, and vice versa when the string is too quiet.

## Jazz Guitar 

### *TOOL LIST*

- ❑ Screwdriver
- ❑ 6" Ruler

1. While holding the strings down by the neck joint, measure the distance from the bottom of the string to the pickup. Measurements may vary based on the type of pickups and a musician's personal preference. Some good middle-of-the-road measurements to get you started are: on the high string side, aim for slightly under 1/8"; on the low string side, aim for slightly over 1/8".

2. Using a screwdriver, adjust the pickup screw. Be aware there are limits on how far the pickup will adjust up or down. You can strip the screw if you tighten too much. If you loosen too far, the screw may detach from the pickup. On a jazz guitar, you're looking for a softer, darker tone as compared to the bright, edgy rock guitar tone. The closer the pickup gets to the strings the brighter the tone.

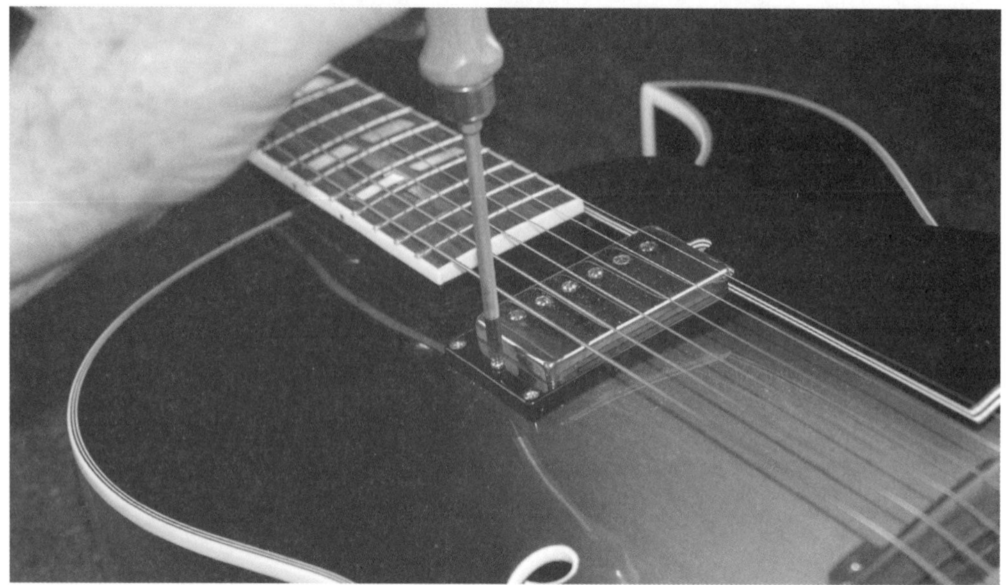

3. Recheck with the guitar plugged into an amplifier, using your ears to adjust. This is subjective, so experiment with the pickup height to find a flavor that fits your style.

TOOLBOX

**Adjusting Pole Preference**

On most guitars with passive humbucking pickups, you can raise and lower the height of the pickup polepieces for individual strings. Doing so will affect the output of the string.

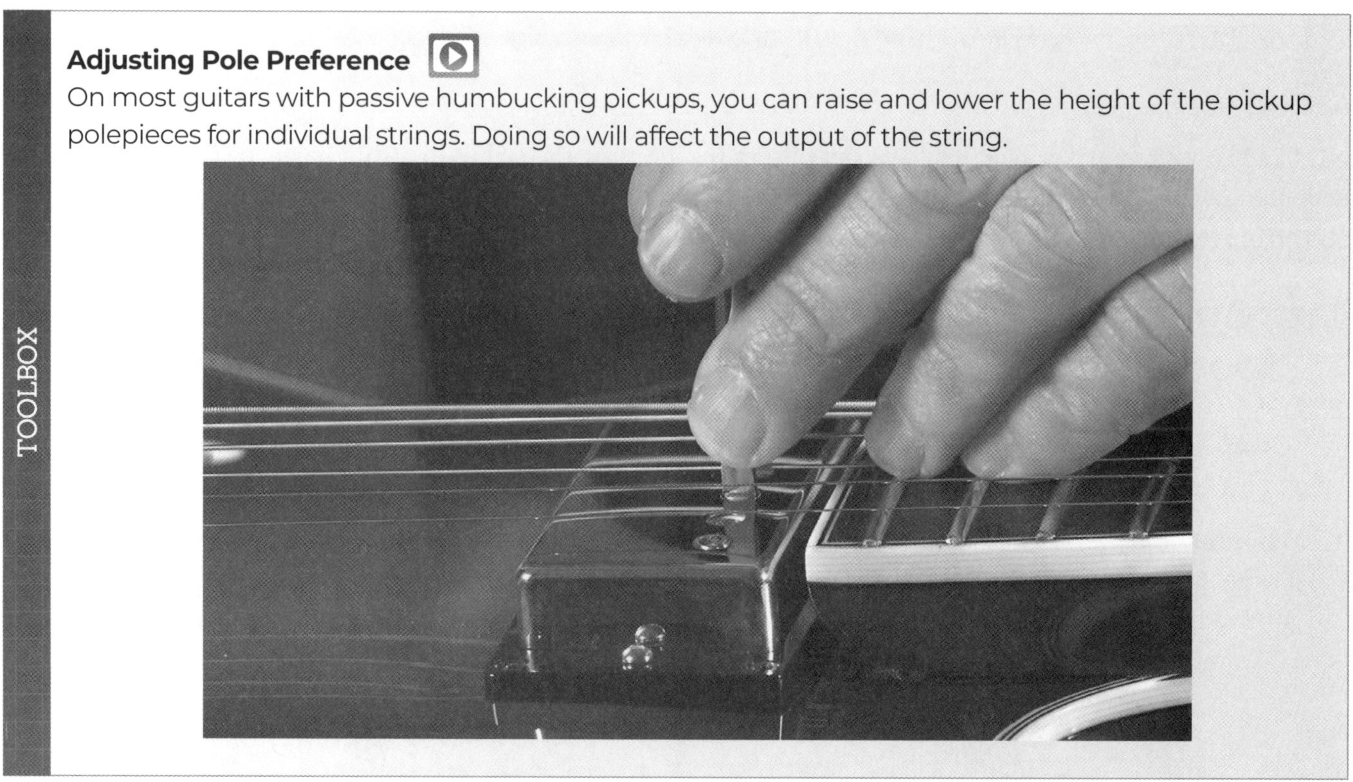

# CHAPTER 7:
# Basic Electronic Modifications

The search for a new sound, deeper bottom, cleaner tone, more distortion, etc. never ends for most guitarists. This is all part of the art of playing guitar, and you can make significant sonic changes with electronic modifications without breaking the bank.

Modifying your guitar's electronics is a way to easily transform your sound. The most common modification is changing the pickups. Companies like Dimarzio, Seymour Duncan, and Frailin Pickups built their brand around replacement pickups.

Changing pickups is just one piece of the puzzle. There are also some wiring modifications that will let you squeeze even more sonic options out of your axe. These modifications are relatively easy to do even if you have no experience with electronics.

## Soldering Basics

### Soldering Tools

Soldering is at the heart of most electronic modifications. You'll need several tools to start soldering:

***TOOL LIST***

- ❏ Soldering Iron (25- or 30-watts)
- ❏ 60/40 Rosin Core Solder
- ❏ De-soldering Pump or Bulb
- ❏ Soldering Iron Stand
- ❏ Damp Sponge

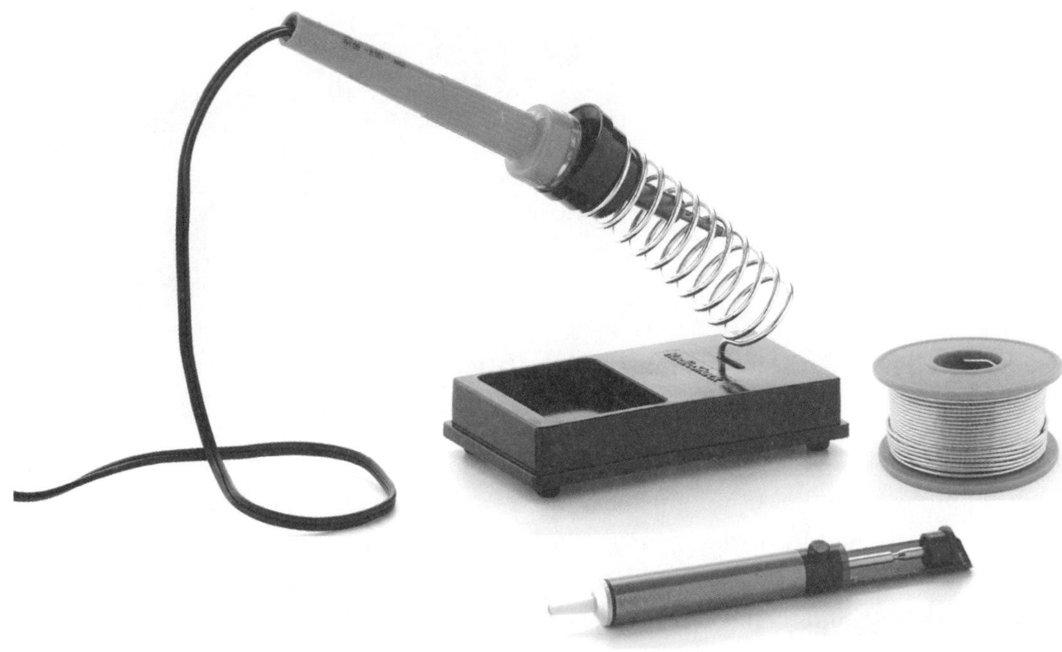

### Soldering Connections

Soldering irons are easy to use but you will need to understand some basics.

1. Plug the soldering iron in and let it heat up for about five minutes. Clean the iron with a wet sponge to remove excess solder off the tip. Be sure the tip is clean and not corroded. You can clean it up with a small file.

2. Once the soldering iron is hot, "tin" the tip of the iron by melting a large amount of solder onto the tip and holding the solder there for 4 or 5 seconds before flicking it off. This allows for a quick heat transfer making soldering quick and accurate.
3. Strip the ends of the wire to create clean wire for soldering connections and create a stable connection with the terminal before soldering. Place the tip of the soldering iron on the connection and immediately apply solder. As soon as the solder flows over the wire and terminal remove the soldering iron. When done properly, making a solder joint is something that takes just a few seconds. Holding the soldering iron in place too long is the most common mistake. Make sure not to jar or move the connection for 4 or 5 seconds after you remove the soldering iron.

## De-soldering Connections

De-soldering is the process of removing solder from existing connections to disconnect wires and prepare terminals for reuse. You'll need a de-soldering pump (solder sucker).

1. Remove wires by holding the soldering iron tip on the connection while lightly pulling on the wire. The wire will release as the solder softens.
2. Clean up the terminals with the solder sucker. With the solder sucker and the soldering iron placed on the terminal together, wait for the solder to soften then hit the button on the solder sucker. Reset the solder sucker and repeat the process until the terminal is clear enough to install new wires. Small amounts of solder remaining is okay as long as you can fit the new wire.

**TOOLBOX**

Before you start a wiring project, take a photo of how the guitar is wired. Most new pickups come with easy-to-read schematics for wiring the pickup but if not, it's helpful to draw your own schematic. A new wiring job can get confusing and it's always nice to have a reference for what you're wiring.

## Stripping Wires

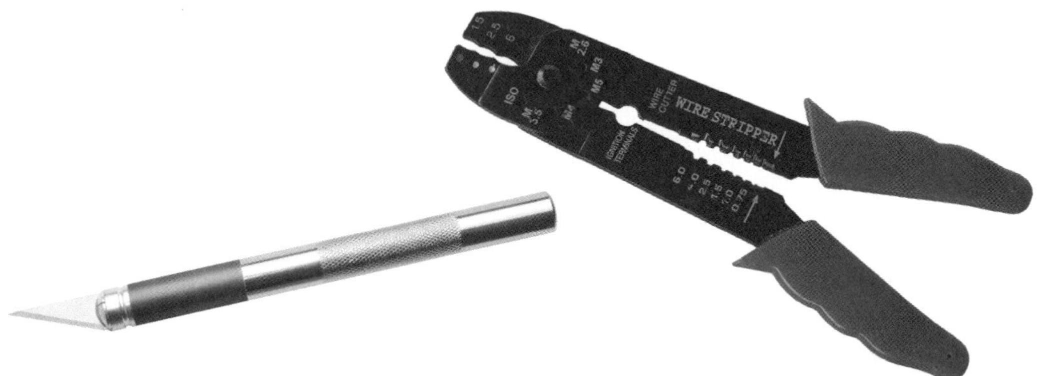


Use wire strippers or an Exacto knife for stripping the insulation from wires. Wire strippers can be set to the size of the wire you're working with. When using an Exacto knife, work with the wire laid out on a surface that you don't mind potentially scratching.

On a typical wiring project, simply cut off a piece of wire, estimating how much wire you'll need. When using a shielding wire, strip a portion of insulation from the ends to expose the shield and core. Separate the shield from the core wires and twist the shield strands together to use as a ground wire. Ensure all ends of the shield wire are together because any stray strands could short out the guitar if they make contact with a hot wire.

In general, it's a good idea to twist the ends of wires together so they are nice and tight without parts veering off in different directions.

# Common Modifications

## Installing a Pickup

Guitar pickups come in a variety of styles from low output to high output, and active or passive. The different types of magnets used in a pickup, like Alnico or Ceramic, also play a part in giving a pickup its unique tonal properties. In this video, I'll replace the bridge pickup to change the guitar's tonal characteristic.

This wiring also requires an on/on/on mini toggle that will allow for series, parallel, and single coil switching with a humbucking pickup that has four colored wires and a bare wire for ground. Typically, humbuckers are wired in series and adding parallel wiring and a coil tap is a great addition to the sound palette of any guitar.

Unfortunately, there is no standard when it comes to color coding, but it's easy to find the coding for your pickup online if you know the brand name.

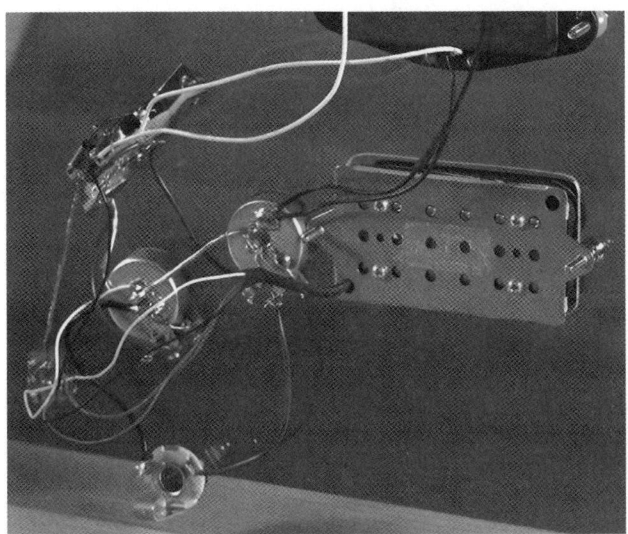

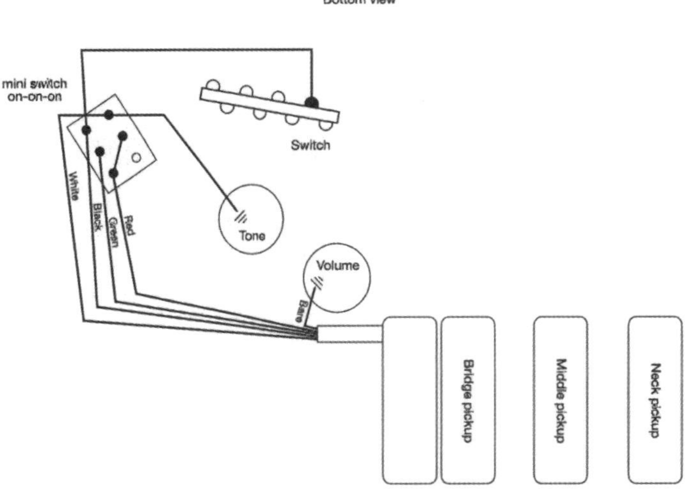

**Screwdriver Test**

After finishing a job, use a screwdriver to test your connections. Plug the guitar into an amp to make sure nothing has shorted out by accident. Touch a pole piece with a screwdriver, listening for sound in each pickup configuration (full humbucker and split coils).

## Tele-style Guitar, Installing a 4-Way Switch

Installing a 4-way switch on a Tele-style guitar to get the pickups wired in series will make your Telecaster sound beefier and louder without sacrificing anything from the three traditional tones. The first three positions will be standard Telecaster switching, and the fourth position (closest to the neck) will be the new series sound with pickups connected in series.

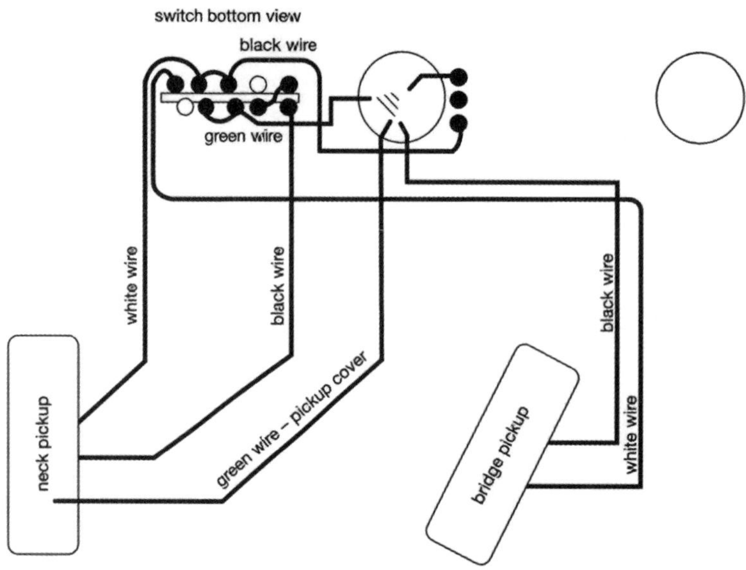


## Treble Bypass

Creating a treble bypass filter on the volume control helps solve the loss of high frequencies when the volume is turned down. The great Chicago blues man, Jimmy Johnson, wouldn't play a guitar unless I wired it up with a treble bypass filter. This modification requires a .001 capacitor and a 120k-150k resistor. The 120k will have the most effect and the 150k will have less effect.

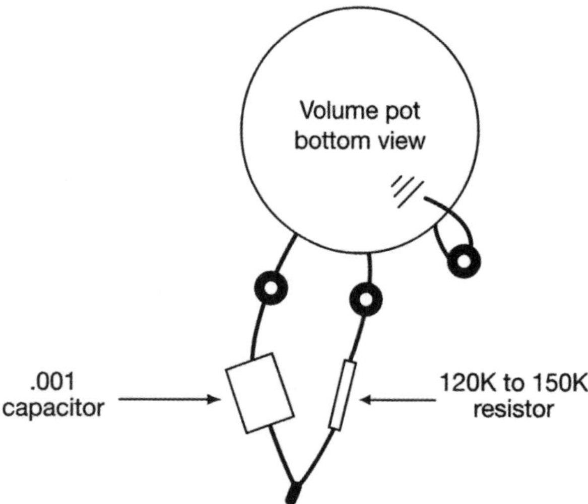


## Shielding

Shielding helps quiet the 60-cycle hum that's inherent with popular single coil pickups. Humbucker pickups are exactly that, the pickup is designed to buck the hum. The design and type of magnets used to make a pickup can eliminate or lesson hum, but it also determines the tonal range and character of the sound it produces.

Single coil pickups remain popular because they have great tone and frequency range. The single coil pickup system is like an antenna, picking up external electromagnetic interference. Shielding helps cancel this interference and quiet the hum. This modification won't eliminate all noise, but when done properly, makes it much more tolerable.

The idea with shielding is that you are trying to encase the electronics to block off interference. The tighter you make the enclosure the better it will work. All shielding needs to be grounded.

TOOLBOX

When plugging into an amplifier, it's important to know what's on that circuit. For instance, if neon lights are on the circuit, it can cause an awful irritating buzz/hum through the speaker. Whenever possible, pick an isolated outlet.

## Places to Shield:

### Pickguard

You can use aluminum or copper tape to shield the pickguard. It is important to understand that all shielding must be "grounded" to work. To ground something, all controls and switch housings must contact the metal tape.

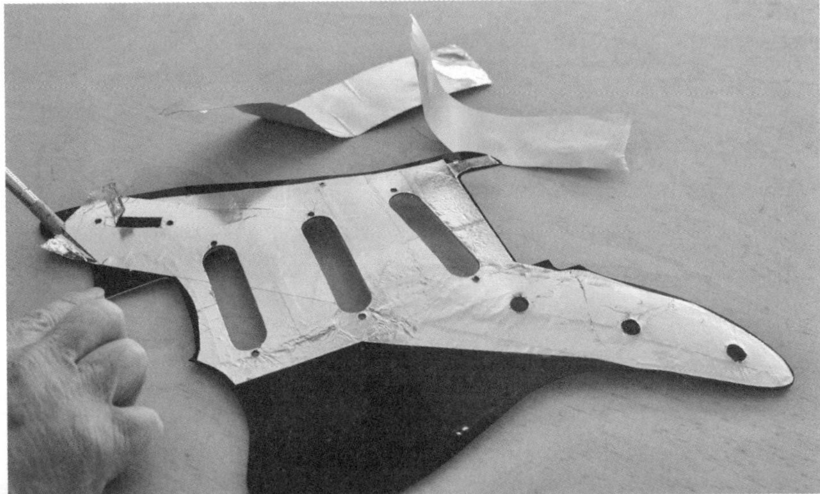

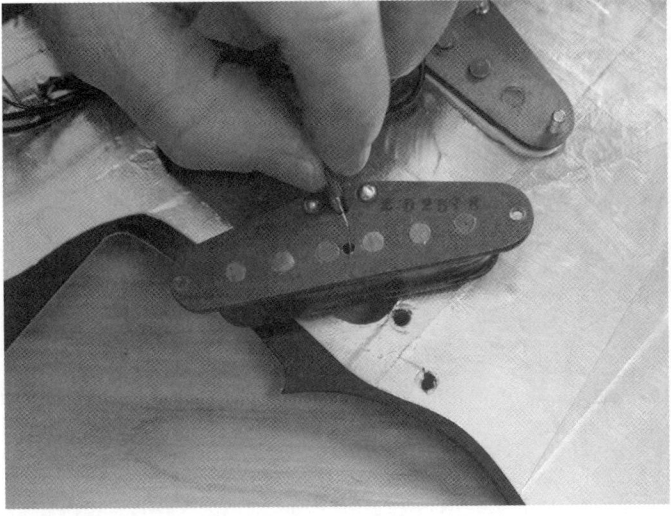

### Body Cavity

The body cavity is done with copper tape or shielding paint. When using copper tape, you will need to solder sections of tape to ensure connection with each other. Leave excess tape folded onto the top of the guitar so it connects with the shielding from the pickguard. Be sure to leave just enough so it is covered by the pickguard. This ensures proper grounding.

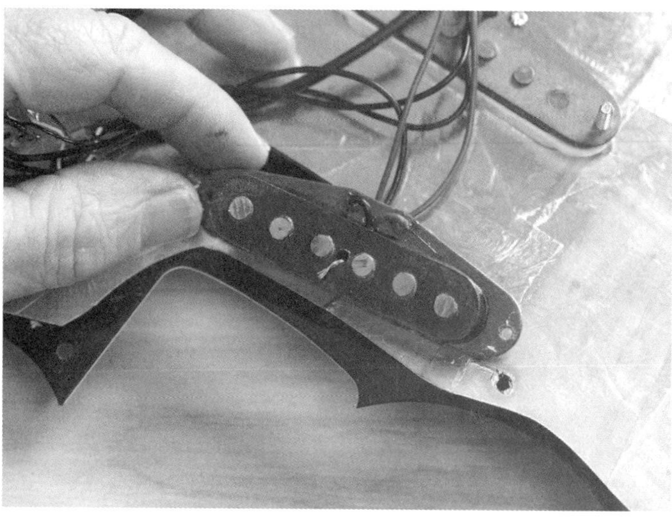

TOOLBOX

Tape edges are sharp so be careful. To avoid cutting your fingers, use a dowel rod to press the tape down.

## Pickup Cover

Shielding paint is best for this job, but if you're good with applying copper tape that will work too. To ground the pickup cover, you will need to have a wire that is soldered to ground connect with the inside of the pickup cover.

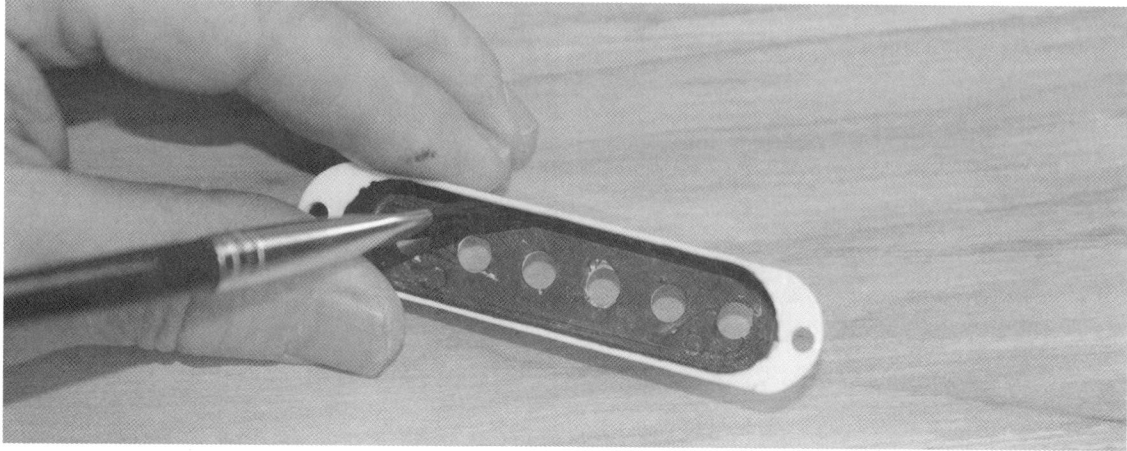

## Jack Cavity

For this area you can use copper tape or shielding paint. Once again, leave excess tape folded onto the top of the guitar so it connects with the metal jack plate to ground the shielding.

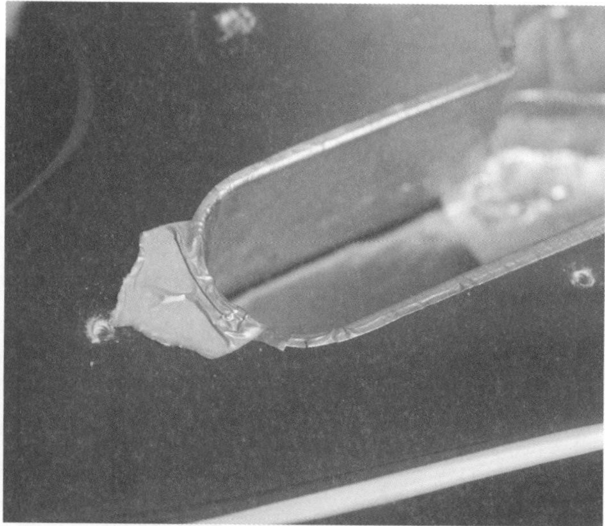

TOOLBOX

It is very important that no positive terminals contact the shielding as it will short out the electronics. Use black tape over the shielding to protect areas that could potentially touch.

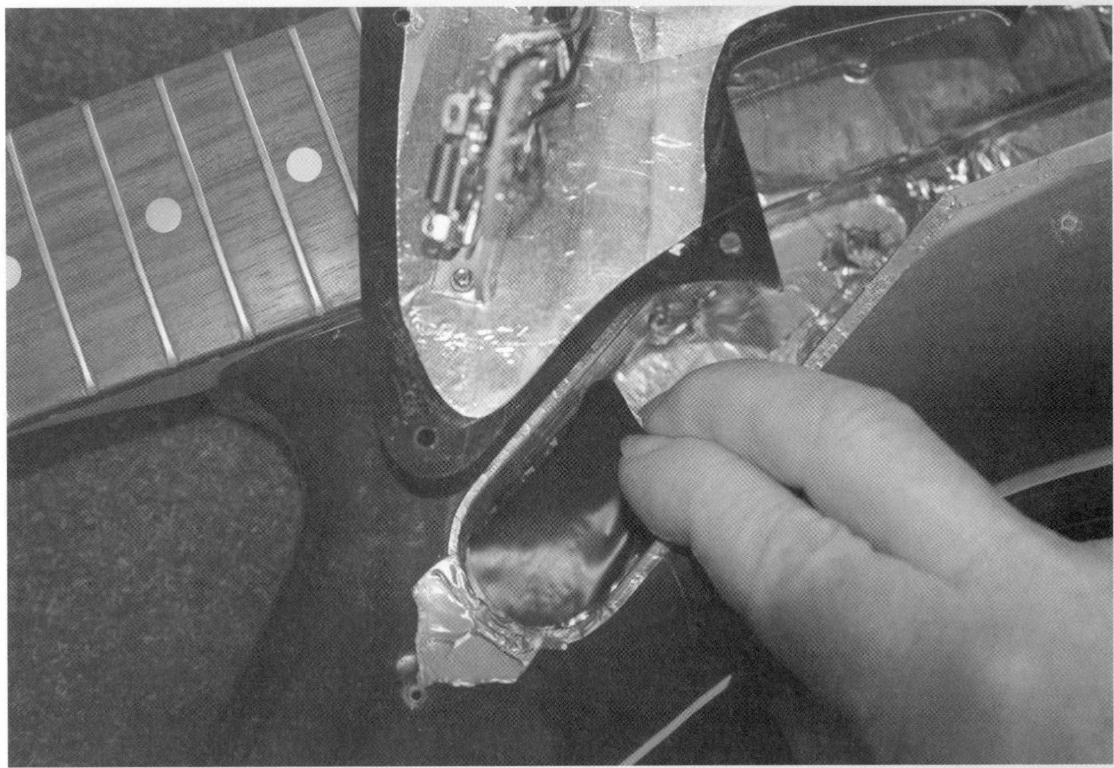

# CONCLUSION

In this book, I have covered important basics to help you understand what you can do to improve the sound and playability of your guitar. These setup and basic modifications can transform your guitar into an instrument that will rival the best of the boutique builds.

Even if you're not mechanically inclined, don't be afraid to try any of the material covered in this book—it's not that hard! As you gain experience, you'll be able to keep your guitars dialed in and playing so comfortably that you can focus solely on making music, which, in the end, is what it's all about!

### ***BONUS VIDEO:*** *Trade Secrets* 

# APPENDIX

## Tools of the Trade

*These tools can be found at your local hardware store.*

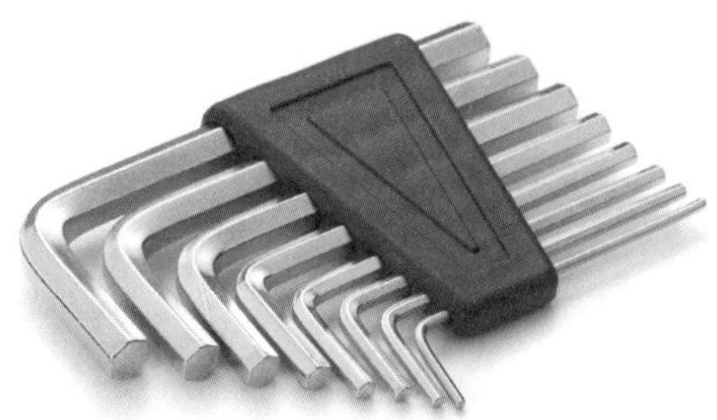

**Allen Wrenches:** For saddle and truss rod adjustments. It's advised to have both a Metric and American standard set.

**Dowel Rod:** Helps with stretching out strings and for securing copper tape.

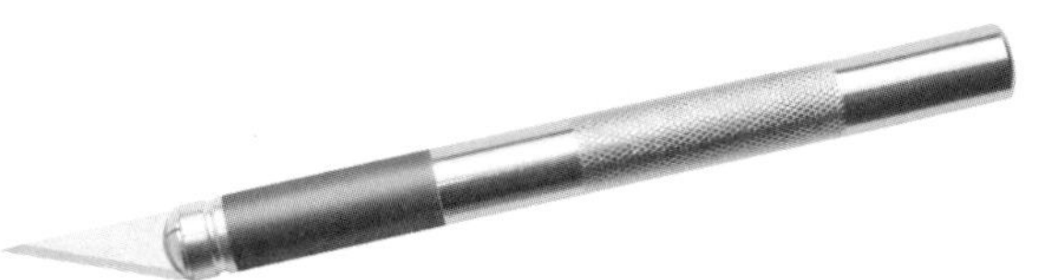

**Exacto Knife:** Used in wiring jobs as well as other miscellaneous tasks like removing excess shim.

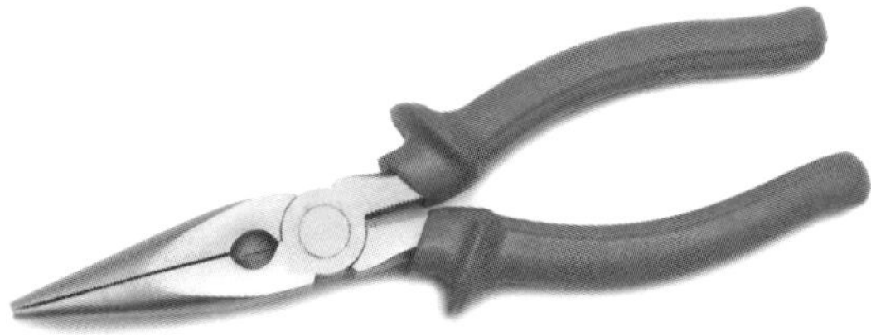

**Pliers:** An all-around tool used in a multitude of jobs. Needle-nose pliers are especially handy when working on electronics.

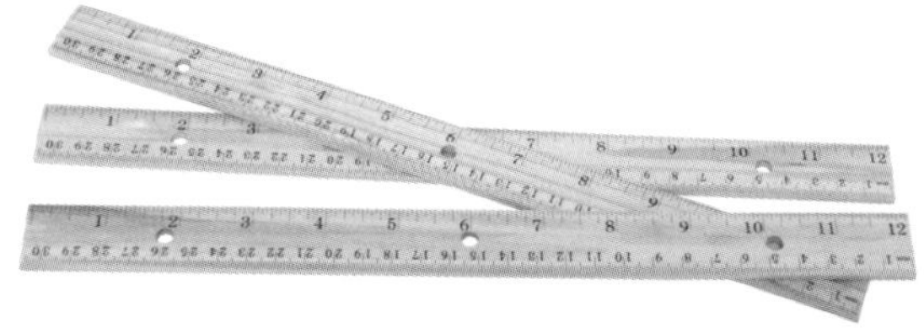

**6" and 18" Ruler:** For taking various measurements.

**Sandpaper:** Have an assortment of grits (80, 120, 220, 600 etc.). A lower grit means the sandpaper is more coarse.

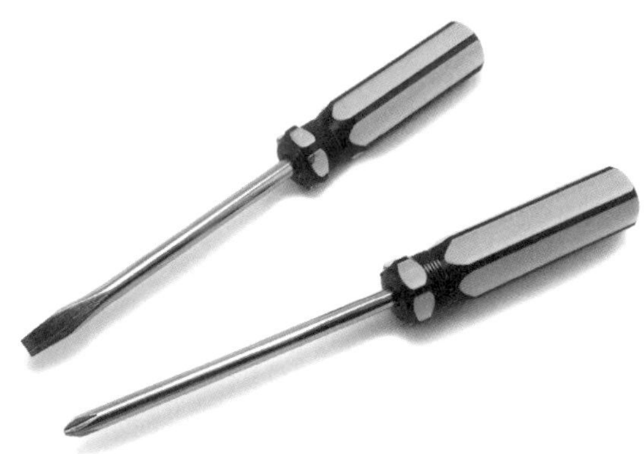

**Screwdrivers (Flathead and Phillips):** Needed for all types of repairs, such as removing pickguards, saddle adjustments, and other miscellaneous jobs. Always keep multiple sizes of screwdrivers on hand.

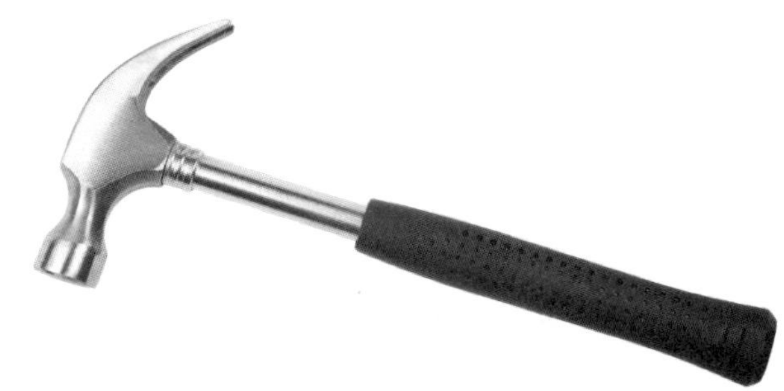

**Small Hammer:** For tasks like removing the nut.

**Teflon Tape:** For alleviating string binding at the nut (and in some cases at the bridge saddles).

*These luthier tools are available at places like Luthier's Mercantile (www.lmii.com) and All Parts (www.allparts.com), in addition to some music stores.*

**3-in-1 Oil:** For lubricating metal parts and preventing rust.

**WD-40:** All-purpose lubricant that can help with loosening a tight truss rod.

**White Glue:** Used in various jobs like adding a shim.

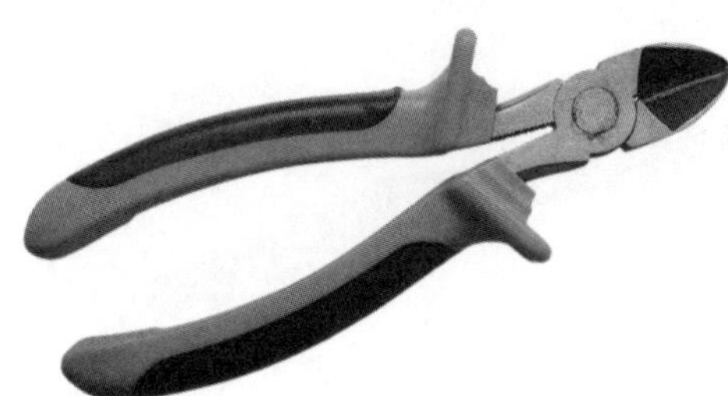

**Wire Cutters:** For clipping excess wire and string ends.

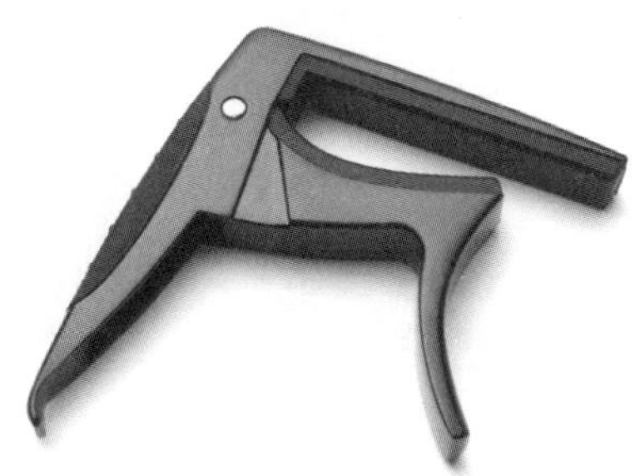

**Capo:** Clamps down strings as you complete tasks such as measuring the guitar's action.

**Guitar Set-Up Mat:** With a built-in neck rest and soft backing material. This offers good support for your guitar as you work.

**Neck Rest:** A foldable neck rest is portable and helpful when you're on-the-go.

**Nut Files:** Come in various sizes that will be close to the gauges of the strings.

**TOOLBOX**

It's a good idea to have a small box to put screws in as you're working. It's very easy for them to get misplaced or fall off the workbench.

**String Winder:** Makes tuning strings easier and quicker.

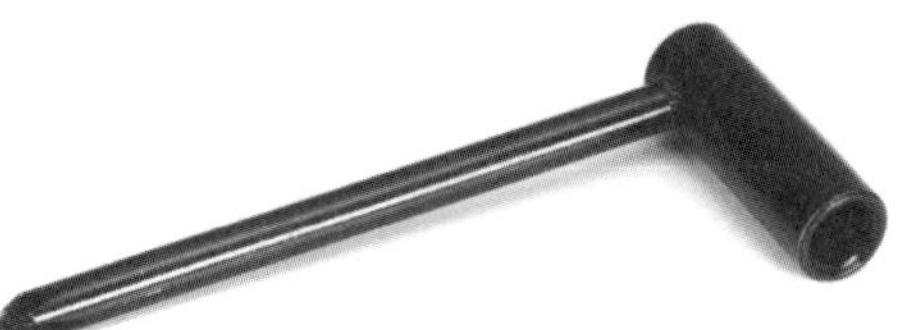

**Truss Rod Adjusting Tool:** Have an assortment of these to accommodate the different truss rods you'll come across.

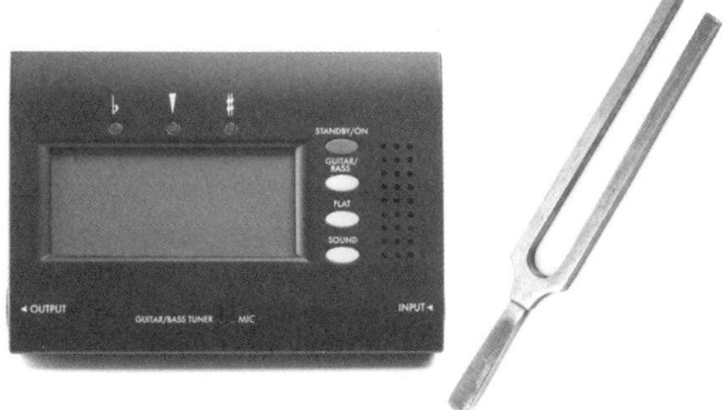

**Tuning Device:** Digital tuners will work but strobe tuners are preferred. Tuning forks, while not a necessity can also serve as a quick reference for pitch.

*These electronic tools can be found online or at your local hobby/electronics store.*

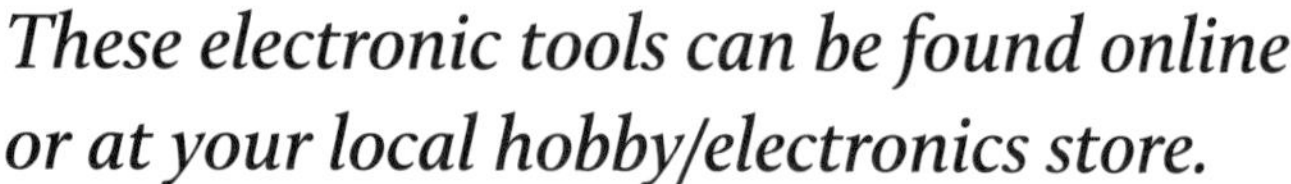

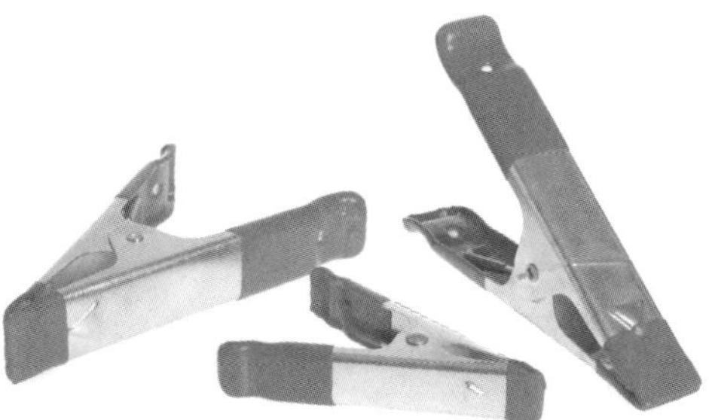

**Clamps:** For holding parts while completing wiring jobs.

**Copper Tape:** For wiring and shielding jobs.

**60/40 Rosin Core Solder:** Used with the soldering iron on wiring and shielding jobs.

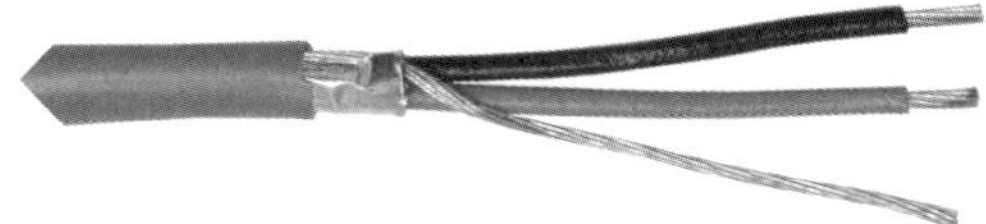

**Shielded Wire:** Required for some wiring jobs.

**30W Soldering Iron and Stand:** For connecting wiring and shielding. The stand often needs to be purchased separately.

**22 AWG Stranded Copper Wire:** These wires come in assorted colors, which is helpful for keeping things organized.

**Wire Strippers:** Required for any electronics repair.

# Do-It-Yourself

# GUITAR SETUP & MAINTENANCE

## BY DENNY RAUEN



To access video, visit:
**www.halleonard.com/mylibrary**

Enter Code
4705-4018-8374-2778

**Video Transcription and Text Editing by Joe Charupakorn**

ISBN 978-1-70518-427-1

Visit Hal Leonard Online at
**www.halleonard.com**

World headquarters, contact:
**Hal Leonard**
7777 West Bluemound Road
Milwaukee, WI 53213
Email: info@halleonard.com

In Europe, contact:
**Hal Leonard Europe Limited**
Dettingen Way
Bury St Edmunds, Suffolk, IP33 3YB
Email: info@halleonardeurope.com

In Australia, contact:
**Hal Leonard Australia Pty. Ltd.**
4 Lentara Court
Cheltenham, Victoria, 3192 Australia
Email: info@halleonard.com.au

# INTRODUCTION

Whether it's replacing a string, adjusting the action and intonation, or even something more complex like changing a pickup, there are fundamental setup and maintenance tasks that every guitarist should be able to do.

In this book I'll cover the basics you'll need to maintain your guitar easily on your own. This will save you time and money—no more long waits and pricey repair bills for a simple turn of the truss rod that will take you five seconds!

Of course, some repairs are beyond the scope of this book, and in those cases, seeking the help of a qualified repairperson is advised. But there are many tasks that anyone—even those not mechanically inclined—can do.

## Online Resources

Using the unique code on page 1, access expert video instruction to get you started on the right foot. Videos are indicated throughout the book with this symbol .

## Guitar Anatomy

Before starting, let's make sure we're familiar with all parts of the guitar.

**Body:** The part of the guitar with the sound hole on acoustic guitars and where the pickups are located on electric guitars.

**Bridge/Tailpiece:** Where the strings are anchored on the body. This is often one component, but with electric guitars the bridge and tailpiece can be two separate parts.

**Fretboard:** Front part of the neck where the frets are located.

**Frets:** Thin metal bars on the fingerboard that separate the guitar into pitches based on the chromatic scale.

**Headstock:** Where the tuners are located at the top of the neck.

**Inlays:** Are a variety of shapes marking the 3rd, 5th, 7th, 9th, 12th, 15th, 17th, 19th, and 21st frets.

**Neck:** Long thin part of the guitar that you put your hand around.

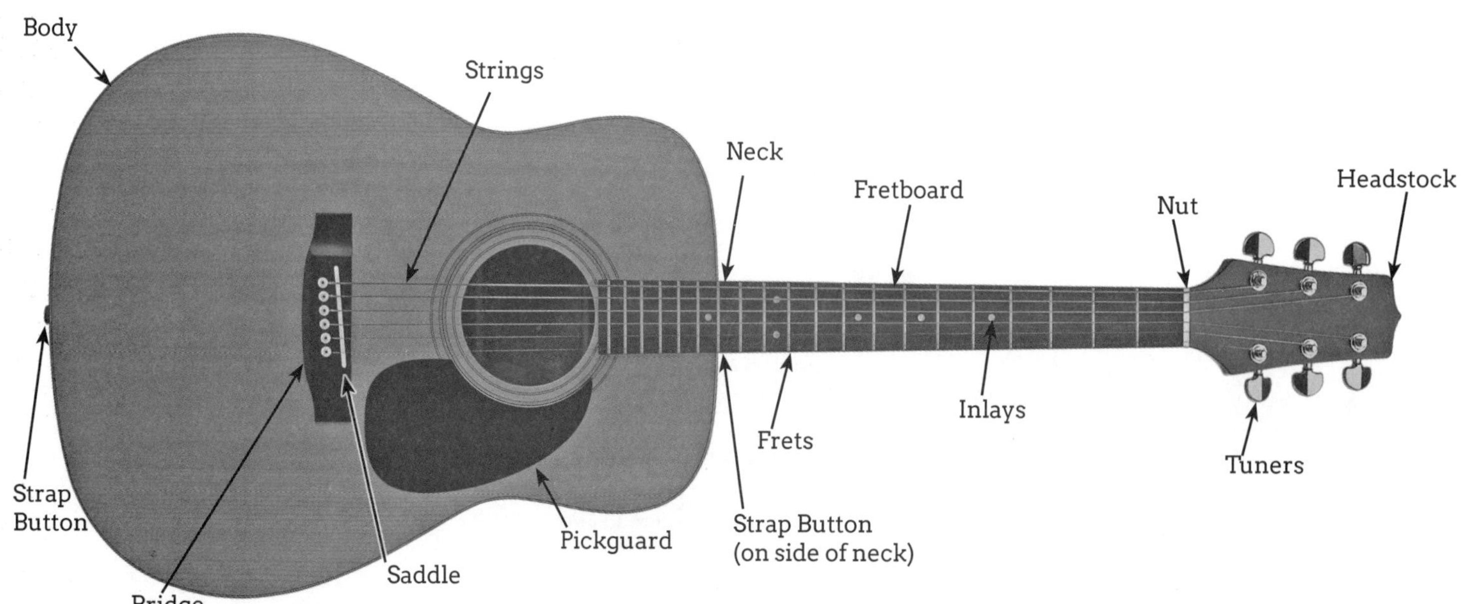